METRO
SAINT ANDRÉ

5E ARR
RUE DE LA HUCHETTE
31
de qualite
Le vrai gout
L'alliance du Gout et de l'originalite
L'instant gourmand
La qualite
le gout du vrai
Le gout, le plaisir et la qualite
FORMULE CLASSIQUE
FORMULE CHAUDE
FORMULE SALADE
FORMULE CONFORT

ARNAUD DELMONTEL

PARIS PÂTISSERIE

70 RECIPES AT THE HEART OF PARISIAN HISTORY

PHOTOGRAPHY
Guillaume Czerw

TEXT
Bénédicte Bortoli

PREFACE
Stéphane Bern

UNIVERSE

RUE
DE TURENNE
DE MUSEES
Cuisine
Maison
Spécialités
de
Viandes

Preface

It would be wrong to think that pâtisserie has only become a genuine passion in France since television began successfully broadcasting *Le Meilleur Pâtissier* ("The Best Pastry Chef") competition in 2012. It's true that many pastry chefs have since become household names—their cakes have made the mouths of millions of sweet-toothed food lovers water on social media, while their store windows attract endless queues. However, for historical accuracy, we must look back to the great reformers of French gastronomy and the promoters of sweet desserts in the 19th century, when sugar ceased being a rare and expensive commodity, only available to the privileged upper classes. Antonin Carême and Auguste Escoffier brought the art of pâtisserie into the modern age, creating new techniques and recipes and radically rewriting the rules. Behind each cake or pastry lies a delicious story, one that excites our curiosity as much as it awakens our longing to indulge ourselves ... and, in so doing, immortalizes the name of those who created it. The towering centerpieces made of choux pastry profiteroles owe their existence to the Croquembouche of Antonin Carême. King Stanislas Leszczynski, the Duke of Lorraine and Louis XV's father-in-law, must have played a large part in inventing madeleines—first made at Commercy by Madeleine Paumier to rescue a failed dessert—just as he helped make Nicolas Stohrer's Rum baba such a success (the latter being the pastry chef who followed Stanislas's daughter Marie Leszczynska to Paris). And who can forget the Financier, which became popular near the Paris Stock Exchange after the pastry chef Lasne brought the little almond cake back with him from the Visitandine order of nuns in Nancy? The same can be said of Italian pastry chef Frascati's Religieuses, Seugnot's Millefeuille, or the Paris–Brest, created by pastry chef Louis Durand in the shape of a bicycle wheel to celebrate the start of the cycle race at the end of the 19th century. So many stories, so many human adventures, recounted and passed on along with the trade secrets that keep legends alive. This beautiful book invites you to take an indulgent stroll through the desserts that recall sweet, and reassuringly comforting, memories of childhood. In it, Arnaud Delmontel pays a huge tribute to Parisian pâtisserie, having taken over a legendary address in the rue des Martyrs that prides itself on having been in existence for 150 years. As a resident for 20 years of the Nouvelle Athènes district of Paris, I have lost count of the number of diversions and detours I've had to make, only to finish up succumbing to the lure of chocolate or lemon cakes, Galette des rois, or Tarte bourdaloue; This latter owes less to the greed of the preacher of kings than to the street named after him in the 9th arrondissement, close to the church of Notre-Dame-de-Lorette, where pastry chef Nicolas Bourgoin of the Lesserteur Pâtisserie created the mouthwatering almond and pear tart. In tribute to the gustatory pleasures of Arnaud Delmontel's pâtisserie, I am delighted to share with you this unashamedly indulgent book.

Stéphane Bern

arnaud
DEL
MON
TEL
A. Delmontel

ARNAUD DELMONTEL

— Parisian pastry chef —

The basics Rolling out, piping, folding, presenting ... these are the skills of a craftsman, the tricks of the trade that are both precise and have to be mastered, which first attracted me to the kitchen and then, very quickly, to pâtisserie. I was trained in the classical traditions of great French gastronomy in the restaurant of the Nikko hotel in Paris, at Mère Blanc in Vonnas in eastern France, at the Les Neiges hotel in Courchevel, at Maison du Chocolat—and even in the kitchens of the Hotel Matignon. I learned my profession at the Rollet Pradier, Gérard Mulot and La Vieille France pâtisseries before flying to the United States and staying for several months, curious to apply my "French touch" to that of American pâtisserie. All these many experiences fueled my desire to develop my own vision of pâtisserie, in my own store.

My place I had always dreamed of having a sign outside a neighborhood store on the corner of a street with a door that you pushed open early in the morning in search of a little treat. Once inside, I wanted my place to be warm and welcoming with customers immediately being greeted with the toasty aroma of freshly baked bread just out of the oven and where, for a few euros, everyone could start their day with a baguette, croissant, or macaron. As soon as I acquired my first store 25 years ago, I decided that I would be a baker *and* a pastry chef, working with flour and mousseline cream, baguettes and galettes. I would be in both the bakery and the development kitchen. This dream was made possible not only with the support of my wife, Valérie, who is the pillar of strength in our family, but also of our children Camille, Paul, and Louis, who were once rocked to sleep lulled with the aromas of baking and who have shared the whirlwind that is our life as artisan entrepreneurs.

(Re)-naissance of a pâtissèrie

In 1999, I took over La Renaissance, a prestigious Parisian institution dating back 150 fifty years. With the keys in my hand and full of doubts and debts, but also dreams and ambitions, never did I imagine that, one day, I would hang a sign with my name on it outside a second, then a third ... followed by even more ... store fronts. By setting myself up at 39 rue des Martyrs in Paris's 9th arrondissement, I was modestly following in the steps of a long line of bakers and pastry chefs who have contributed so much to the story of our national pâtisserie profession and to the gastronomic prestige of our city and its international reputation. When Monsieur Beaumont, who owned the property in 1874, wrote on the wall of his small store "deliveries made to addresses in the city", there was no way he could have imagined that one day I would be delivering my baguettes beyond the Boulevard de Clichy—and even to the Élysée Palace!

Paris, right bank

This cosmopolitan capital, this City of Light, is my territory, my place of work, and my playground. I was born here, I live here, and I bake here. Paris has become my laboratory. And not just any Paris! The one of artists, painters, writers, poets, and street performers. A bohemian and creative Paris that never stands still, just like our profession. Returning to the rue des Martyrs, where I created and sold my first "Arnaud Delmontel" breads, cakes, and pastries, it is impossible for me to forget that more than a century ago, we might have spotted Beaudelaire, Daudet, the Goncourt brothers, Monet, Pissarro, Courbet, Bizet, Hugo, or Ravel, sitting at tables in a bistro or brasserie nearby. This 885-meter-long street is the district's heartland, the symbol of a Paris that is forever vibrant and inspiring, a breeding ground for talent. Even today, the fertile imagination of my colleagues and the diversity of what Parisian pâtisserie has to offer are a source of stimulation. I am proud to honor this city of culture and character, which continues to embrace the world around it.

A house dedicated to craftsmanship and family

When, five years after taking over La Renaissance, I opened another store on the rue Damrémont and then five years later a third on the Rue de Lévis, still in the center of Paris, each time I felt as though I had to scale Everest once again by recreating myself and my image in another place with another team. Over the years we have worked hard to create a company that is genuinely family-run and operates on a personal scale. I live with my family close to my stores and I am proud to be able to count on colleagues who have been with us for more than 20 years. Together we have lived through both difficult times and moments of great joy. I would like, without any grand gestures, to leave my mark, showing that with hard work and passion, everything is possible!

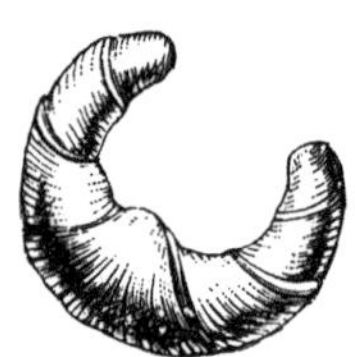

"An artisan of little pleasures"

This is how I define myself. It may seem a little naïve but it is a reflection of the values I hold close to my heart: those of indulgence, joy, and simplicity, through making handcrafted creations as good to eat as they are beautiful to look at. Our cakes and Viennese pastries permit us to enter the intimacy of our customers' homes, both on a day-to-day basis and also for festive occasions. We bring cheer to a family's Sunday lunch or a buffet party on a special day. And yet I do believe that these "little pleasures" have a big role to play.

Big and small stories

School didn't inspire me, but history certainly did! I have always loved being surrounded by books and collecting old, battered volumes devoted to pâtisserie. I have built a collection of traditional recipes that first appeared in Paris such as Paris–Brest, Opera, Saint-Honoré, and Tarte Bourdaloue. Sometimes their provenance and their history are uncertain, but to me their flavor is the very essence of Paris. These recipes are the ones I learned in the great houses that trained me and the ones I have since refined myself and passed on to the 150 apprentices who have worked in our stores over the last 25 years, all part of the virtue of passing on knowledge. From one generation to the next, we never stop reimagining standard recipes, making these timeless classics our own, and calling them "the pastry chefs' greatest hits". In this book, I would like to salute the knowledge, talent, and inventiveness of the artisan bakers and pastry chefs of Paris. It is a living and vibrant tribute to my profession and an invitation to experience my gourmet Paris by biting into the best!

Simple, delicious and honest

That is how my cakes and pastries look. I like flavors to be clean and identifiable, for a sensory experience that is as direct as possible. My aim is to serve the best, in a way that combines a respect for tradition with new innovations. A creativity that's filled with joy and with little twists that never fail to challenge my regular customers. Innovation comes from collaborations, which most often are the result of meetings with other artists in my neighborhood, perhaps following a discussion on the corner of a bar counter. That's my Paris, too, a mix of the arts and by learning from others.

Taste, above all else

Taste, of course, is all about using quality products, bought from trusted suppliers that I remain loyal to, some of which are personal friends. It is also about sourcing produce as locally as possible, something that is more difficult with pâtisserie than it is with bakery. Today, three-quarters of the raw materials we work with are manufactured within a 200-kilometer radius of Paris. The taste comes from a natural levain (sourdough starter) that gives our signature breads a distinctive flavor, in particular our "Renaissance" loaf, which won us the Grand Prix de la baguette de Paris in 2007.

— Contents —

Greater Paris
Montmartre
Pigalle
Opéra
Palais-Royal
Châtelet
Latin quarter
METRO

THE MOUTHWATERING HISTORY OF PARISIAN PÂTISSERIE

PÂTISSERIE:

Dough prepared, seasoned, and baked in the oven; Profession, trade of pastry chef; Place where pastries are made.

Paris and pastry chef are words that send gourmets into reveries and make the mouths of the entire world water. As the capital of culinary delights, Paris has always been the benchmark for trends and innovations in pâtisserie. One of the world's leading cities and a communications hub where food from every corner of the country arrives by land and river, it has absorbed influences from elsewhere and shared that knowledge. So, let's look at the gourmet history of this mecca of gastronomic hedonism and sophistication.

CEREALS, SEEDS, AND WATER

Could a flat bread drying on stones in the sun and made since Neolithic times, be a basic predecessor of our breads and pastries today? With the development of agricultural crops and improved tools to harvest them, this grain-based dough has survived for centuries and through civilizations. From ancient times, the Greeks and the Romans decorated it with aniseeds, coriander seeds, and poppy seeds, before sweetening it with fruits and honey, Honey was the only food "sweetener" used until sugar was discovered at the beginning of the first millennium—a sweet flavor so special and sacred that, until the Middle Ages, it was primarily an offering to the gods.

THE FIRST PÂTISSIERS

Originally it was *oblayers* (also called *oublayers* or *oublayeurs*) who made oblates—a sort of sacrificial bread—as well as *fouaces* (a brioche-style bread often flavored with orange blossom water), flatbreads made from fine flour and baked under ashes, and *buignetz* (beignets) with apples, figs, pike, rice, curd, or sage. They also prepared cooked creams, crackers, custards, and cakes based on beans. In the 18th century, *pastillarii* (pastry chefs) and *pistores* (bakers) sold their savory and sweet bakes in the street. At that time, they were one of the oldest guilds established in Paris and enjoyed a special status. In fact, the *Livre des métiers de Paris* (The book of Parisian trades) mentions exemptions for pastry chefs. These included their rights, of course, but also the increasingly strict rules governing many things including hygiene, quality control, and fair pricing, which were all governed by a strict moral code. An *oublayeur*-pastry chef must have received "neither wicked blasphemy nor complaint" and an "unmarried female *oublayère* is forbidden to take on a male apprentice"!

With the Crusades, cane sugar arrived in the West and the technique of rolling and folding dough, which was already known to the Greeks and Romans, became widespread. Pastry bases had arrived.

FROM PÂTÉS TO DESSERTS

Until the 16th century, pastry chefs made and sold meat, fish, and cheese pâtés seasoned with different condiments, but also tarts and filled *flancs* (pies), small choux, brioches, and *talmouses* (cheese fritters). What all these things had in common was that they were made from a dough and were usually cooked. These food artisans, who were among the most numerous of all trades, contributed to the capital's renowned gastronomic reputation, having to feed an urban population that was equally numerous.

It was not until the 15th century (1440) that the guild of pastry chefs acquired its own set of regulations and the exclusive right to make pastry. Some professionals, such as *pain d'épice* (gingerbread) makers, had their own regulations. From the start of the next century, pastry chefs specialized in sweet dishes (the *pistores dulciarii*) and "high quality pastries" using the finest ingredients (such as wheat from quality white flours, selected cheeses and eggs, Isigny or de Gournay butter and spices) and, as a result, began to stand apart from meat and fat merchants. "Sweet" was gaining social recognition. In 1566, the statutes were revised, extended, and stabilized, establishing a well-organized practice for a community that was both powerful and united until the guilds were abolished by Turgot.

In Paris, the majority of pastry chefs had settled in the same street (rue des Oublayers) to which they had given their name. They hung a lantern on their store signs, which they lit each evening, while their colleagues in the southern provinces placed two large tin vases on either side of their stores.

LUXURY, REFINEMENT, AND ABUNDANCE

Having settled in Paris, chefs who cooked for the royal tables added to the capital's prestige and power. For Anne de Bretagne's supper (Louis XII's second wife), various pâtés, sweet tarts, and "other mysterious things from the oven" were served. At the time, the "dessert," (sweet things such as pastries, jams, confectionery, and liqueurs), came at the end of the meal. The star cake, *pain d'épice* (gingerbread), demonstrated the widespread use of honey as a sweetener. While the Italians had been growing sugarcane in Sicily for two centuries and mastered the process of refining it, in France, cane sugar was still an expensive commodity to import. If Catherine de Medici has been credited with all kinds of culinary revolutions, she is certainly the person to thank for elevating the pleasures of the table through bringing to court highly skilled Italian cooks, pastry chefs, confectioners, and ice cream makers. As a result, during the reign of Henri II, palates became more refined as pastry recipes became more complex. And we are still enjoying macarons, pralines, genoise sponge cakes, and ice creams today!

Various cakes from *The Book of Pâtisserie* by Jules Gouffé.

"Entre les mets"

In English this means "between the courses," an expression now condensed into a single word, entremets. As the name suggests, entremets once referred to a pause or break for entertainment after each course, before eventually coming to mean a modern dessert. An entremets was originally a small dish or sweetmeat (jam or other confectionery) eaten after the roast. In Ancient Rome, chilled drinks were served at banquets during interludes for musical entertainment. These small dishes coming "between the courses" were common in France and Italy until the end of the 16th century. In 1694, the first edition of the *Dictionnaire de l'Académie française* gave a more precise definition: "what is served on the table after the roast and before the fruit; usually made up of ragouts." Today, the word entremet is most commonly used to describe a cold dessert. However, "*entremetier*", the title given to a chef de partie in charge of preparing vegetables, pasta, eggs, soufflés, and sauces, also refers to savory dishes. Nowadays, only a few of the top gastronomic restaurants include an "*entremétier*" among their kitchen brigade.

THE FIRST REVOLUTIONS IN PÂTISSERIE

When she married Louis XIII in 1615, Anne of Austria brought chocolate with her as part of her dowry and it revolutionized confectionery. Cocoa imported from the Americas often reached France via Spain, sometimes taking indirect routes through other ports. The 17th century was also when some key discoveries were made, such as organic yeast from hops, but also technical advances in the conservation of food, as well as advances in pâtisserie creations. Recipes for Chantilly cream, crème pâtissière, choux pastry, apple turnovers, madeleines, and croissants were invented or at least recorded for the first time in culinary repertoires. It was a creative time that continued into the next century with the arrival of refrigeration, advances in cooking methods, and the advent of mechanization (such as machines for crushing cocoa and kneading doughs). New utensils were also developed such as the pastry wheel, saccharometer, and alcoholmeter. By the 18th century, pâtisserie had become so refined that it remained the preserve of the privileged few. The splendor of the royal tables stood in stark contrast to widespread famines and shortages, often accompanied by bans on producing luxury pastries and breads.

PARIS, THE EARTH MOTHER OF FRANCE

The work carried out by Louis XIV's minister Colbert and his successors ensured a continuous supply of the best regional produce to the capital. Local specialities began appearing and making their mark, eager for recognition. The stores in Paris were full of produce that came from all parts of the country and seduced the Parisians. Pâtisserie did not escape the trend. Under the Ancien Régime, Paris was the undisputed capital of taste, where culinary trends and "good manners" were reported in magazines like the *Mercure galant*. It was in the heart of the city, and not at Versailles, that chefs made their name and set trends. Reputations were made, with the publication of more and more cookbooks that shared recipes and techniques. These books, which celebrated the latest ideas and trends, heralded the beginning of a culinary literature that would increase during the 19th century.

In the 18th century, confectionery was a demanding profession, with know-how being passed from generation to generation. At that time, confectioners had begun mastering how to make chocolate bonbons and pastilles with a thousand flavors, plus *diablotins* (soft chocolate caramels) and other sought-after sweets. Pecquet, a sweet maker in the rue des Lombards who supplied Louis XV, pioneered the technique of coating *dragées*, in the same way as it is done today. In grand houses, these tiny works of art would be stored in chocolate and confectionery boxes. The height of sophistication was to nestle them in a pocket-sized box made from a precious material such as gold, silver, ivory, or rare wood.

PLACES OF CULINARY DEBATE

The arrival of cafés in Paris, places where people could eat but also debate, followed by the opening of restaurants, helped fuel the excitement that was surrounding this culinary art and they came to symbolize the elegance of Parisian life.

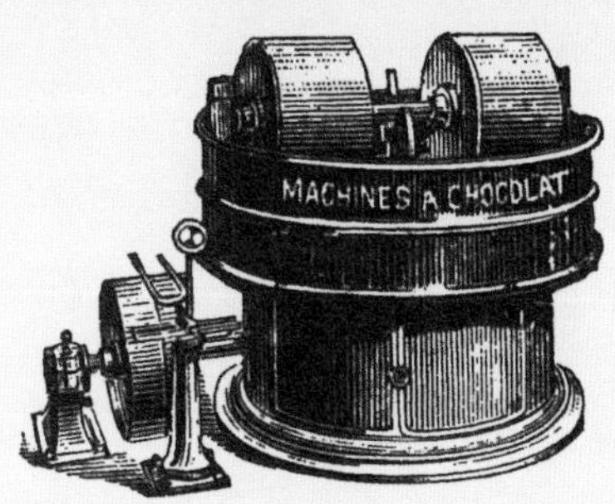

THE GOLDEN AGE OF PÂTISSERIE

The 19th century marked the highpoint of French pâtisserie—a period when the craft was not only formally defined but also opened up to unprecedented levels of creativity. Technical progress—from the creation of the first coal-fired oven to the cocoa grinder and the manufacture of new tools and utensils such as the whisk, the sugar spinner, and pastry cutters—encouraged inventiveness and the development of new recipes alongside elegant decorations. According to Antonin Carême, Parisian stores selling fine pâtisserie multiplied from 258 in 1815 to 352 in the 1870s, as well as around 210 baker–pastry chefs who supplied cafés with not just bread but also croissants, and 176 "*darioleurs*" making brioches, galettes, puff pastries, baked custards, filled pastries, and other popular items. Another factor that helped pâtisserie become more mainstream was beet sugar, which was refined in France or near its borders; this was much more accessible both economically and geographically than cane sugar (see page 16).

"À la parisienne"

In the 19th century, the term "à la Parisienne" (Parisian-style) began appearing in cookery books. It mainly referred to elaborate dishes, but ones without any particular regional identity or that required special skills and specific ingredients, unlike dishes "à la Normande" or "à la Provençale", which featured regional produce or local traditions. Recipes "à la Parisienne" are more a combination of everyday dishes created in family kitchens and then refined and made more international by famous chefs to be served in top restaurants.

STARS OF PARIS

The great Parisian pastry chefs named their stores after themselves and added their signatures to their elaborately decorated creations. Techniques were refined and fashions followed one after another. Every ambitious pastry chef who was eager to get ahead had to be in Paris. Names began to be talked of and creations started to be attributed to the men or their stores. Examples of this were Rouget, the "Montmorency of the oven", in the rue Saint-Honoré ; Bailly, rue Vivienne, where Antonin Carême worked before opening his own store in the rue Napoléon (today the rue de la Paix) and famed for his ramekins and grilled choux; Stohrer, in the rue Montorgueil; Chiboust, in rue Saint-Honoré, famous for the cream bearing his name and the basis of the gâteau Saint-Honoré; Gouffé, a pupil of Carême, in this same street and "master of ornamental pâtisserie"; the Julien brothers in rue Vivienne, for their savarin; Quillet, rue de Buci, for his meringue flan and so on ... It was the golden age of towering *pièces montées* created in architectural form and cakes with English-inspired decorations that elevated them to works of art. Pecquet, a confectioner and supplier to Louis XV, was based in the rue des Lombards, as were most of his colleagues, but there were also a number of stores selling precious objects, as well as art dealers, indicating that confectionery was undeniably a luxury item.

Guides recommended *"bonnes maisons"* which, since the French Revolution, were no longer just for the aristocracy. Pastry chefs like Carême, Grimod de La Reynière, and Gouffé theorized the art of pâtisserie, offering advice to young professionals and setting out their vision for the profession.

According to Carême, the modern pastry chef, must be both an architect and a designer, be gifted with "perfect taste, have an inventive imagination and industrious fingers". Both a craft and an art, pâtisserie was thought out and formalized.

The Sugars

Since ancient times, honey had been used to sweeten dishes, galettes, sauces, and drinks. It was also used medicinally in the preparation of syrups and ointments. For centuries, cakes had been predominantly sweetened with honey or by adding dates or grape juice. Sugar cane, which for a while had been mistaken for a "honey cane" had been eaten in India for millennia to reduce the acidity of certain dishes. But it wasn't until the 18th century that it was added to cakes, and then coffee and tea, which were fashionable drinks. At the beginning of the century, sugar, which had only just been refined, was sold by apothecaries at a very high price. Pastry chefs, therefore, used brown sugar before the Italians introduced their white sugar from Sicily and before the plantations in the Antilles supplied France.

From 1806, Napoleon's continental blockade led to a shortage of cane sugar and it became necessary to find sugar from other sources. The cultivation of sugar beet was in development and soon became a necessity. In the 1830s, on the outskirts of Paris, the Say and Lebaudy refineries began making sugar from sugar beet grown in northern France. Less expensive, this new ingredient helped make pâtisserie available to all.

A Feast for the Eyes

Parisian breads and pastries had traditionally been made in full view, without showmanship or flourishes, but now they were protected from public curiosity behind glass. Store signs were given a makeover, and were now adorned with mirrors, ceramic tiles, and stained glass. It brings to mind Cadine, Zola's heroine in *Le Ventre de Paris* (The Belly of Paris), published in 1873, who in the book shows a "great fondness for the Taboureau bakery, where a whole window had been dedicated to cakes and pastries" and in front of which she returns "ten times, to walk past the almond cakes, Saint-Honorés, savarins, flans, fruit tarts, plates of babas, cream-filled éclairs [...] overwhelmed by the jars full of biscuits, macarons and madeleines" in this "very bright baker's shop with its big windows, marble surfaces, gilding and wrought-iron racks for bread [...]" It recreates perfectly the diversity of the products offered by Parisian pâtisserie stores and the elegant and eye-catching way they were presented—a combination of the best and the beautiful. In this way, and through friendly rivalry, the most sought-after pâtisseries in the capital set themselves apart from other food businesses.

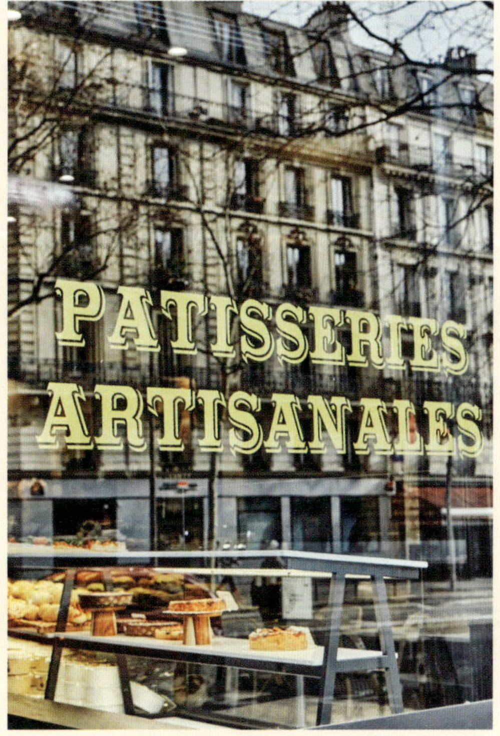

Grand ballroom buffets by Antonin Carême.

"THE CULINARY TOWER OF BABEL"

This phrase, borrowed from Curnonsky and Marcel Rouff, in *La France gastronomique: Guide des merveilles culinaires et des bonnes auberges françaises* (1921), testifies to the ability of Paris to devour and digest regional and foreign influences. Paris was, and is, universal, rich in the produce of the Île-de-France area but also enthusiastic about the specialties of regional France and more "exotic" cuisines. The city had been modernized, remodeled by Haussmann and transformed by electrification. Between 1855 and 1900, Paris hosted five world fairs and visitors from the around the globe came in their millions to enjoy the aesthetic and gastronomic pleasures of Europe's capital of culture.

A period of restrictions and rationing arrived with the Second World War and the pâtisserie stores closed. "No more babas", reported *Paris Midi* in its edition of the 3 March 1941. "The chocolate éclair is banned from entering, the cherry pie cast into oblivion and the cream-filled choux puff banished. Not even the *petit four* has escaped the decree." After Liberation, first the Parisians, and then all of France, returned to the soothing pleasures of the table.

TECHNICAL INNOVATIONS

Mechanization, conservation, regulation. The 20th century saw the challenges of heating and refrigeration mastered. Increased productivity was brought about by the widespread use of machines to undertake tasks such as kneading and rolling that had previously been done manually. The automation of processing cocoa beans directly contributed to the success of chocolate, there was use of new materials—such as plastic wrap (cling film) and aluminum foil—and increasingly strict hygiene rules and standards for both industrial and artisan breadmaking and pâtisserie were introduced.

A SHOWCASE FOR PÂTISSERIE WITHOUT BORDERS

As pâtisserie became more international, technical and artistic innovation accelerated alongside it. The appreciation of manual skills has been raised and competitions are held to display the skills of French craftsmen and women. In 1929, the *Société des Meilleurs Ouvriers de France* (Best Craftsmen in France Association) was created and, 60 years later, came the first *Coupe du Monde de la Pâtisserie* (World Pastry Cup). Showcasing French pâtisserie, Paris plays host to national and international teams and events, celebrating its execution, taste, and creativity. The good and the beautiful have never been so visible, amplified by social media platforms that break audience records and bring unprecedented media attention to the chefs.

Prolific and endlessly creative, Paris remains the birthplace of gastronomy and, as a result, of a pâtisserie tradition that embraces modern times while honoring and continuously exploring its rich heritage.

THE LANDMARKS OF FRENCH PÂTISSERIE

IT IS OFTEN DIFFICULT TO DETERMINE THE EXACT DATE A RECIPE WAS CREATED AND TO BE CERTAIN OF ITS PROVENANCE. WAS THE PERSON WHO RECORDED THE RECIPE THE ONE WHO CREATED IT AND, IF NOT, WHICH OF THEM MADE IT FAMOUS? EVEN TODAY, THE CONCEPT OF PÂTISSERIE CREATION REQUIRES A CERTAIN DIFFIDENCE.

▶ **1533:** macarons first brought to the French Court.

▶ **About 1540:** creation of choux pastry attributed to Popelini, the fictional Italian pastry chef of Catherine de Medici at the French Court.

▶ **About 1630:** invention of puff pastry (made with butter) by the painter/pastry chef Claude Gellée, known as Le Lorrain.

▶ **1638:** almond tartlets created by Ragueneau, pastry chef at the Palais-Royal in Paris.

▶ **1645:** organic yeast first added to breads and cakes.

▶ **1660:** whipped cream invented by Vatel, chef to the Grand Condé.

▶ **1720:** invention of meringue attributed to Swiss pastry chef Gasparini.

▶ **1740:** first nougat made by Joseph Michel and the baba introduced into France by Stanislas Leszczynski.

▶ **About 1750–1774:** Menon, inventor of the chocolate biscuit and chocolate mousse, was the first to give quantities in his recipes and to transcribe recipes for *bouchées à la reine* (vol-au-vents filled with chicken and veal sweetbreads) and *allumettes au fromage* (cheese straws).

▶ **1772:** invention of spun sugar by Sabatier, pastry chef to Louis XV.

▶ **1805:** invention of decorative piping by Lorsa, a Bordelais pastry chef.

▶ **1815:** publication of *Pâtissier royal parisien* (The Royal Parisian Pastry Chef), written by Antonin Carême: the first book to give a detailed description of the profession. He also created or updated many recipes (such as soufflé, bavarois, croquembouche, and vol-au- vent) and perfected the technique for making puff pastry.

▶ **1830:** invention of the ice-cream machine.

▶ **About 1860:** ganache created.

▶ **1879:** first appearance of chocolate yule logs (*Bûches de Noël*).

▶ **1910:** Paris–Brest created by Louis Durand, inspired by the Paris–Brest–Paris cycle race.

▶ **1919:** first professional courses offered to apprentice confectioners.

▶ **1924:** first ice-cream making factory opened in France.

▶ **1971:** L'École Lenôtre opened at Plaisir (Yvelines) by Gaston Lenôtre, the face of modern pâtisserie, which has trained several generations of pastry chefs.

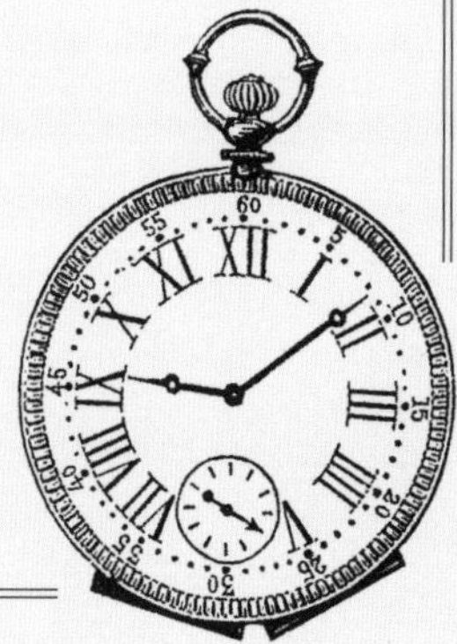

BATEAUX-MOUCHES
LA FLUTE

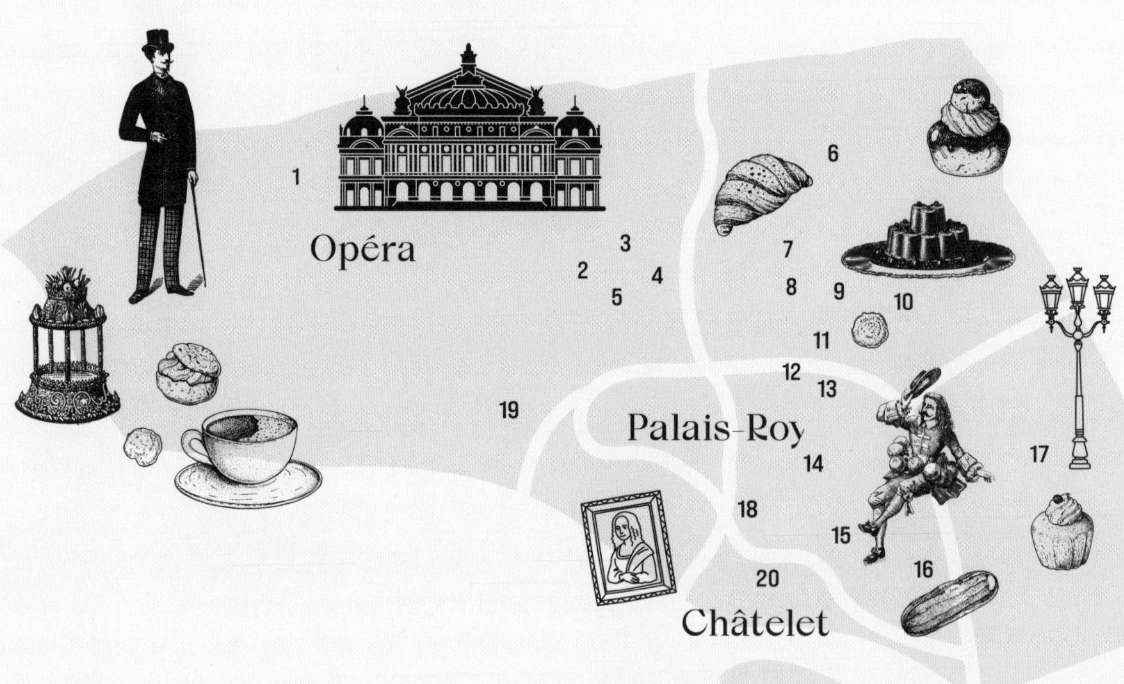

1 —— Opera
2 —— Baked Alaska
3 —— Croque-monsieur
4 —— Boudoir biscuits
Blancmange
Diplomat with glacé fruits
Parisian chocolate charlotte
5 —— Chocolate ganache tartlets
6 —— Religieuses
7 —— Croissants
8 —— Three brothers' cake
9 —— Savarin
10 —— Financiers
11 —— Parisian Savoy sponge cake
12 —— "Failure" cake
13 —— Parisian flan
Croquembouche
Chouquettes
Soufflé
Choux buns filled with Chantilly cream
14 —— T artines Véfour
15 —— Amandine
16 —— Carolines
17 —— Rum babas
18 —— Genoese bread
Saint-Honoré
19 —— Conversations
Chiboust tart
20 —— Marcelin

Opéra, Palais-Royal, Châtelet

Parisian pastry chefs have drawn inspiration as much from the hustle and bustle of the rue Saint-Honoré as from the quiet atmosphere of the rue Vivienne—and revolutionized pâtisserie in the process. While Antonin Carême piled up choux buns to create his majestic "*pieces montées*", Nicolas Stohrer perfumed the air of the Les Halles district with his rum babas. Others, like Charles Dalloyau, were inspired by the grandeur of the Opéra Garnier to create the mythical dessert of the same name. Here in the historic heart of Parisian pâtisserie, architectural monuments sit alongside monuments to Parisian pastries and cakes, often even sharing their name.

•

Preparation time:
1 hour 30 minutes
Chilling time:
Several hours
Cooking time:
6 to 7 minutes

•

INGREDIENTS
TO SERVE 8 TO 10

Joconde sponge

5½oz (150g) whole eggs
1 cup (5½oz/145g) powdered (icing) sugar
1½ cups (5¼oz/145g) ground almonds
4¾ tbsp (1½oz/40g) all-purpose (plain) flour
¼ cup (2oz/55g) butter, melted
4½oz (130g) egg whites
1 tbsp plus 2 tsp (¾oz/20g) superfine (caster) sugar

Buttercream

(⅔ cup less 2 tsp (4½oz/125g) superfine (caster) sugar
5½oz (155g) egg whites
1¾ cups (14½oz/410g) softened butter
Coffee flavoring

Opera

Make the Joconde sponge

Preheat the oven to 425°F (220°C/Gas mark 7).

Fit a stand mixer with the whisk attachment and beat the eggs, powdered sugar, and ground almonds on medium speed for 4 to 5 minutes. Sift in the flour and fold it in, followed by the melted butter. Transfer this mixture to a separate bowl, wash and dry the stand mixer bowl and whisk attachment. Add the egg whites and superfine sugar to the clean bowl and whisk until standing in firm peaks. Using a spatula, gently fold the two mixtures together. Spread the batter over a baking sheet lined with parchment paper in an even layer, ¼ inch (5mm) thick, and bake for 6 to 7 minutes.

Make the buttercream

Put ½ cup (4½oz/125g) water and the sugar in a saucepan over a medium heat and cook until the sugar dissolves and the temperature of the syrup reaches 244°F (118°C). In the bowl of a stand mixer fitted with the whisk attachment, whisk the egg whites until standing in firm peaks. Add the syrup in a slow, steady stream, whisking constantly on medium speed until the syrup has been incorporated. Cut the butter into small pieces and still mixing on medium speed, gradually add the butter until you have a smooth buttercream. Add the coffee flavoring, to taste. Chill in the refrigerator until ready to use.

•

Recipe continues on next page

•

The history of this elegant dessert cake with its glossy, perfectly smooth icing, is full of twists and turns. The story begins with the *Clichy*, a cake created by Louis Clichy, who sold his business and gave the recipe for his favorite cake to Marcel Bugat, one of whose brothers-in-laws worked for Dalloyau. Sensing the Clichy cake's potential to become a crowd-pleaser, in 1955, Cyriaque Gavillon, a chef at Dalloyau, came up with a variation of the recipe, calling it Opéra. Shortly afterward, one of Dalloyau's stores was bought by none other than Gaston Lenôtre, who took the credit for inventing the recipe. As to its name, is it a reference to the shape of the Paris Opera Garnier stage or does it pay homage to the company's dancers, all faithful Dalloyau customers?

Ganache

1 cup (8fl oz/240ml) whipping cream (35% fat)

5½oz (155g) bittersweet (dark) chocolate (70% cacao), chopped

⅓ cup (2¾oz/80g) butter, diced

Syrup

½ cup less 1½ tbsp (2¾oz/80g) superfine (caster) sugar

1½ tbsp (½oz/15g) freeze-dried instant coffee

2 tsp (⅓fl oz/10ml) sugarcane juice rum (optional)

Icing

4½oz (125g) bittersweet (dark) chocolate (60% cacao)

4½oz (125g) brown fondant icing

¼ cup (2fl oz/60ml) neutral oil (such as grapeseed)

A little edible gold leaf, for decoration

Make the ganache

Heat the cream in a saucepan over a high heat. When it boils, pour it over the chopped chocolate and mix with a spatula, gradually adding the diced butter, and stir until the ganache is smooth.

Make the syrup

Bring 7 tbsp (3½fl oz/100ml) water and the sugar to the boil in a saucepan. Add the freeze-dried instant coffee, mix well, then take the pan off the heat. Leave to cool before adding the rum.

Make the icing

Melt all the ingredients together in a water-bath, taking care not to let the mixture get too hot.

To assemble the Opera

Cut the sponge into three squares, each measuring 6 x 6 inches (15 × 15cm). Place one of the squares upside down on a piece of cardboard (the side that was on top during baking goes underneath). Brush it very lightly with syrup and spread two-thirds of the buttercream in an even layer on top. Cover with a second layer of sponge and brush it generously with syrup. Spread the ganache over the sponge. Cover with the third sponge layer and brush that also with syrup. Cover it with the remaining buttercream, spreading it in a very smooth layer. Chill in the refrigerator for several hours.

Cover the Opera cake with the warm, melted icing, spreading it over with a spatula using long, smooth strokes to obtain an even result. You can reserve a little of the icing to coat the sides of the cake, if you wish. Decorate the top of the cake with tiny pieces of edible gold leaf.

AFE DE LA PAIX
CAFÉ de la PAIX
PAIX
RESTAURANT CAFÉ de la PAIX
CAFÉ de la PAIX

Preparation time:
20 minutes
Resting time:
½ day
Cooking time:
20 to 25 minutes

EQUIPMENT

8 tartlet pans, 2½ inches (6.5cm) in diameter
3¼-inch (8.5-cm) round pastry cutter

How one makes tartelettes amandines:
Beat, until they are mousse-like,
Several eggs;
Slowly fold into their mousse:
Juice from your chosen lemon:
Then pour on
Sweet almond milk.

In *Cyrano de Bergerac* (act II, scene 4), the pastry chef Ragueneau recites the recipe for making Amandines. Edmond Rostand's character, who runs a store in the Palais-Royal, was inspired by Cyprien Ragueneau, Cardinal Richelieu's pastry chef. Apart from this scene in the play, no one actually knows who created the recipe!

Amandine

INGREDIENTS
FOR 8 TARTLETS

12oz (350g) sweet tart pastry (see page 131)
4¼oz (120g) redcurrants or cherries in syrup
1 cup (2¾oz/80g) flaked almonds
5½oz (150g) apricot jelly or apricot glaze
Butter for the tartlet tins

Almond cream

½ cup (4¼oz/120g) softened butter
½ cup plus 2 tbsp (4¼oz/120g) superfine (caster) sugar
1¼ cups (4¼oz/120g) ground almonds
4¼oz (120g) eggs, beaten
2⅓ tbsp (¾oz/20g) all-purpose (plain) flour
2 tsp (⅓fl oz/10ml) sugarcane juice rum
Seeds from 1 vanilla bean

For decoration (optional)

8 candied (glacé) bigarreaux cherries
8 small pieces of angelica

Make the sweet tart pastry, cover it in plastic wrap (cling film) and leave it to rest in the refrigerator for half a day.

Make the almond cream

Fit a stand mixer with the whisk attachment and beat the butter and sugar together on low speed. Add the ground almonds and then the eggs, a little at a time. Continue to beat until you have a smooth mixture, scraping down the sides of the bowl as necessary using a pastry scraper or spatula.

Next fold in the flour, rum, and vanilla seeds. Set aside at room temperature.

To assemble and finish

Preheat the oven to 350°F (180°C/Gas mark 4).

Roll out the pastry ⅛ inch (3mm) thick and cut out eight rounds using the pastry cutter. Lightly butter the tartlet pans and line with the pastry rounds, trimming off any excess pastry. Prick the pastry bases with a fork.

Drain the syrup from the redcurrants or cherries. Divide them between the pans and then, using a spoon or a piping bag fitted with a plain tip, cover with the almond cream. Sprinkle over the flaked almonds, then bake the tartlets in the oven for 20 to 25 minutes. Leave to cool before turning the tartlets out.

Heat the apricot jelly or glaze in a small saucepan and brush it over the tartlets. Decorate each one with a cherry and a small piece of angelica, if using.

CAFE BAR

Although small, crescent-shaped cakes were already being made in 17th century Paris, it was not until 1770 that they were introduced to the French court by Marie-Antoinette. In 1830, two Austrians were selling *kipferls*, croissants made with brioche dough, at their Viennese boulangerie on the rue de Richelieu. In 1905, this king of Viennese pastries had a flaky texture and by 1920 the croissants were being made with butter. At this point, they became a fixture on the breakfast tables of the nobility and the bourgeoisie.

Croissants

Preparation time:
30 minutes
Resting time:
3 hours
Cooking time:
10 to 15 minutes

INGREDIENTS TO MAKE 20 CROISSANTS

3¾ cups (1lb 2oz/500g) strong white bread flour
2½ tsp (⅓oz/10g) salt
5 tbsp (2oz/60g) superfine (caster) sugar
1 tbsp (½oz/15g) acacia honey
1½ cups plus 2 tbsp (12oz/350g) unsalted butter
¾oz (20g) baker's (fresh) yeast
1 cup (8½fl oz/240ml) whole milk
2 eggs, for glazing

Fit a stand mixer with the dough hook attachment and put the flour, salt, sugar, honey, and 7 tablespoons (3½oz/100g) of the butter in the bowl. Mix the yeast with the cold milk, add to the bowl and knead the ingredients together on slow speed for 2 to 3 minutes, followed by 7 minutes on medium speed. The dough must be smooth and elastic. Shape the dough into a ball, cover it in plastic wrap (cling film), and leave it to rise for 30 minutes at room temperature.

Using a rolling pin, flatten the dough into a square and chill it for 30 minutes. Transfer the dough to a work surface. Place the remaining butter on top in the center, flatten it with the rolling pin and wrap the dough around to enclose the butter. Roll out the dough to a rectangle measuring about 24 x 12 inches (60 × 30cm).

Give the dough three turns, usually a double turn and a single one, chilling the dough for 30 minutes between each turn. Roll out the dough to a rectangle ⅛ inch (4mm) thick and measuring 20 x 10 inches (50 × 25cm). Cut the dough into 20 triangles and roll each one up from the base toward the point. You can lightly stretch your rolled out dough to make a croissant with more turns that will be flakier when baked.

Transfer the croissants to a baking sheet covered with baking parchment. Leave the croissants to rise for about 1 hour until they have doubled in volume.

Preheat the oven to 400°F (200°C/Gas mark 6).

To make the glaze, beat the eggs together in a ramekin and brush over the croissants. Bake for 10 to 15 minutes until golden brown.

EIN
CASA • CAPASA
Menu Cocooning
CAFÉ ARTISANAL
CAFÉ GRAIN
CAFÉ MOULU
SACHET DE COLDBREW
MONODOSES JAPONAISES
NAAD COFFEE

Open
Lemon Cake

•
Preparation time:
30 minutes
Resting time:
12 hours
Cooking time:
1 hour
•

EQUIPMENT

5½ to 6¼-inch (14 to 16-cm) pastry ring, 1¾ inches (4.5-cm) high

Parisian flan

This *flan pâtissier* (baked custard) is the perfect example of the skills of baking and pâtisserie coming together. In medieval times, breads and *'flans'* were baked side by side in ovens and in his book, *The Royal Parisian Pastry Chef*, the great Antonin Carême mentions the *flan Parisien*, which looks identical to the *flan pâtissier* but has a pastry case. There are two schools of thought over whether the pastry should be there. The *Parisien* is better suited to having a crisp base but, without question, it is its success in the capital's store windows that make it quintessentially Parisian!

INGREDIENTS
TO SERVE 6 TO 8

Shortcrust pastry

1¾ cups plus 2 tbsp (9oz/250g) all-purpose (plain) flour, plus extra for dusting
5 tbsp (2oz/60g) superfine (caster) sugar
A dash of natural vanilla flavoring
¼ cup (2oz/60g) butter, cut into small pieces
1oz (30g) egg
Butter for the pastry ring

Flan filling

2 cups (17fl oz/500ml) whole milk
1 cup plus 3 tbsp (9½fl oz/270ml) whipping cream (35% fat)
1 vanilla bean, slit lengthwise and seeds scraped out
3oz (85g) whole eggs
2¼oz (65g) egg yolks
¾ cup (5½oz/150g) superfine (caster) sugar
⅓ cup (1½oz/40g) cornstarch (cornflour)

Make the shortcrust pastry

Sift the flour onto a work surface and make a well in the center. Add the sugar, vanilla flavoring, and butter and, with your fingertips, work everything together to make a crumbly dough. Add the egg, mixing again without kneading the dough. Flatten the dough with the palm of your hand and push it away from you to make it smooth.

Shape the dough into a ball, flatten it, and cover in plastic wrap (cling film). Let it rest for several hours in the refrigerator. Remove the dough from the refrigerator and roll it out on a lightly floured surface. Butter the pastry ring, stand it on a baking sheet, and line it with the pastry. Trim the edges and chill.

Make the flan filling

Heat the milk and cream in a saucepan over a medium heat. Add the vanilla bean and the seeds.

Whisk the eggs, egg yolks, sugar, and cornstarch together. Pour in a little of the hot milk and cream and mix, then pour the mixture back into the saucepan. Stir constantly until the custard returns to the boil. Preheat the oven to 375°F (190°C/Gas mark 5).

Remove the vanilla bean (the bean can be rinsed and then used again). Pour the warm flan into the pastry case and bake for 1 hour. Leave it to cool then chill in the refrigerator for a minimum of 2 hours, which will make the flan even better.

Parisian Savoy
sponge cake

Among the Savoy sponge cake recipes, the one from Pâtisserie Félix, a grand 19th century house in the rue Vivienne, is one of the very best.

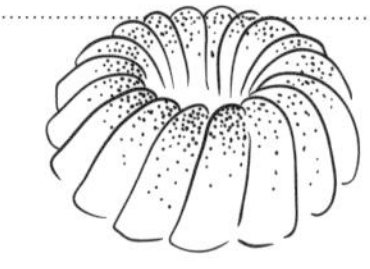

•

Preparation time:
20 minutes
Cooking time:
45 minutes

•

EQUIPMENT

Savoy cake or Genoese sponge pan, 10½ or 11¼ inch (26 or 28cm) in diameter

INGREDIENTS TO SERVE 8

14 eggs
2½ cups (1lb 2oz/500g) superfine (caster) sugar
Seeds from 1 vanilla bean
1 ⅓ cups (6½oz/185g) all-purpose (plain) flour
1¾ cups (6½oz/185g) cornstarch (cornflour)
1 pinch of salt
Butter and sugar for the cake pan

Preheat the oven to 375°F (190°C/Gas mark 5). Butter the pan and dust it with sugar.

Separate the eggs into whites and yolks.

Put the sugar, vanilla seeds, and egg yolks into a mixing bowl. Beat with an electric mixer fitted with the whisk attachment until the batter is very creamy and has become pale and thickened.

Sift the flour with the cornstarch, then whisk into the cake batter.

Whisk the egg whites with the pinch of salt until standing in firm peaks. Fold them into the batter using a spatula, mixing gently until they have been evenly incorporated.

Pour the batter into the pan, filling it by two-thirds. Bake for 45 minutes. Check if the cake is cooked by pushing the tip of a sharp knife into the center; the knife must come out clean.

Turn the cake out onto a wire rack.

A very 'French' recipe said to have originated at Le Véfour, a gastronomic mecca that has played host to Paris's political and artistic elite for more than two hundred years. Tucked under the Palais-Royal arcades, Victor Hugo, Honoré de Balzac, George Sand, Colette, Jean Cocteau, Napoleon, and Josephine, are just a few of the legendary figures who dined there and are remembered on the tables bearing their names.

Tartines Véfour

Preparation time:
1 hour 30 minutes
Cooking time:
8 to 10 minutes

EQUIPMENT

Genoese sponge pan or square pastry frame, with 12-inch (30-cm) sides

INGREDIENTS TO SERVE 8

Buttercream ¾ cup plus 1 tbsp (5¾oz/160g) superfine (caster) sugar • ⅔ cup (5¼fl oz/160ml) water • 2½oz (75g) eggs • 1 cup plus 3 tbsp (9¼oz/265g) butter, cut into small pieces • 1 tbsp (½oz/15g) coffee flavoring

Genoese sponge 5½oz (150g) eggs (about 3 eggs) • ½ cup less 1 tbsp (3¼oz/92g) superfine (caster) sugar • ⅔ cup (3¼oz/92g) all-purpose (plain) flour

Syrup 7 tbsp (3½oz/100ml) water • ½ cup (3½oz/100g) superfine (caster) sugar • ½ tsp (2.5g) coffee flavoring

Make the buttercream

Dissolve the sugar in the water in a saucepan over a high heat. Boil until the temperature of the syrup reaches 248°F (120°C). Fit a stand mixer with the whisk attachment and beat the eggs on high speed, adding the syrup in a thin, steady stream. Whisk for 2 to 3 minutes, then lower the speed and add the butter. Whisk for a few more minutes. Add the coffee flavoring.

Make the Genoese sponge

Preheat the oven to 350°F (180°C/Gas mark 4).

Place a stainless steel bowl in a water-bath, add the eggs and sugar and whisk until the mixture is warm and mousse-like. Remove the bowl from the water-bath and, using an electric hand whisk, continue whisking for 7 to 8 minutes until the mixture is completely cold. Lower the speed and continue to whisk for 10 minutes. The mixture must be very light and form a ribbon when it falls from a spatula.

Sift in the flour and fold it into the batter using a spatula. Once it is evenly mixed in, pour the batter into the sponge pan or square pastry frame placed on a baking sheet and bake for 8 to 10 minutes.

Make the syrup

Bring the water and sugar to the boil over a medium heat to make a syrup, then take the pan off the heat and whisk in the coffee flavoring.

To assemble

Line a board with parchment paper and place the sponge on it. Brush the warm coffee syrup over it. Stir the buttercream with a whisk to soften it, if necessary. Spoon the buttercream into a piping bag fitted with a ½-inch (12-mm) tip and pipe lines or rosettes on top of the sponge. Cut into 2 x 6-inch (5 × 15-cm) bars. Chill in the refrigerator until ready to serve.

ESTAURANT
VEFOUR
80
CAFÉ
AURANT
FOUR

Financiers

•

Preparation time:
20 minutes
Cooking time:
12 minutes

•

EQUIPMENT

8 financier molds

INGREDIENTS
TO SERVE 8

⅓ cup (2¾oz/80g) butter
⅓ cup (1½oz/40g) ground almonds
6 tbsp (2oz/55g) powdered (icing) sugar, sifted
6½ tbsp (2oz/55g) all-purpose (plain) flour
4½oz (130g) egg whites
3 tbsp (1½oz/40g) acacia honey
Seeds from ½ vanilla bean
Butter for the molds

These little cakes could only have become a daily must-have treat in the Bourse district of Paris! Customers of Paul Lasne's store, most of them financiers, were quickly won over by these small almond-flavored sponges. The shrewd pastry chef chose the name financier for this adaption of visitandines from the Lorraine, baking them into the shape of a gold ingot.

Preheat the oven to 425°F (210°C/Gas mark 7). Butter the financier molds.

Make a brown butter by heating the butter in a saucepan over a medium heat. Leave until the butter melts and becomes foamy. Continue to cook until the foam disappears and the butter becomes amber-colored with a light hazelnut aroma. Take the pan off the heat immediately and filter through a sieve lined with a muslin cloth.

Stir the ground almonds, sifted powdered sugar, and flour together in a mixing bowl. Add the egg whites, brown butter, and honey, followed by the vanilla seeds. Mix well.

Spoon the batter into a piping bag fitted with a ½-inch (12-mm) plain tip and fill each mold three-quarters full with it.

Bake for 12 minutes. Turn out the financiers when they come out of the oven.

This pâtisserie, with its links to the Enlightenment, would have been created to mark the publication of *Conversations d'Émilie* (*The Conversations of Emily*) by Madame d'Épinay in 1774.

Conversations

•

Preparation time:
40 minutes
Resting time:
30 minutes
Cooking time:
30 to 35 minutes

•

EQUIPMENT

3¼-inch (8-cm) round pastry cutter
8 molds, 2 inches (5cm) in diameter and ⅝ inch (1.5cm) high

INGREDIENTS TO MAKE 8

14oz (400g) classic puff pastry (see page 230) • Butter for the molds

Almond cream 3 tbsp (1¾oz/45g) butter • ¼ cup less 1 tsp (1¾oz/45g) sugar • ½ cup (1¾oz/45g) ground almonds • 1¾oz (45g) eggs • 3½ tsp (⅓oz/10g) all-purpose (plain) flour • 2 tsp (⅓fl oz/10ml) rum • Vanilla flavoring, to taste

Royal icing 2 egg whites • 1¾ cups (9oz/250g) powdered (icing) sugar

Roll out the puff pastry ⅛ inch (3mm) thick and cut out 16 rounds using the pastry cutter. Cut strips from the pastry trimmings, ¼ to ½ inch (5mm to 1cm) wide.

Butter the molds. Line them with the eight pastry rounds, pricking the bottom of each with the tines of a fork. Let the pastry overhang the sides of the molds so that you can fix the pastry tops in place once the almond cream has been piped or spooned in.

Make the almond cream

Fit a stand mixer with the flat beater and mix the butter and sugar together on low speed. Add the ground almonds and then the egg. Continue beating, scraping down the sides of the bowl with a dough scraper or spatula to ensure the batter is evenly combined. Add the flour, rum, and vanilla flavor and mix well.

Spoon the mixture into a pastry bag fitted with a ½ inch (12-mm) plain tip (or use a spoon) and fill the tart cases with it.

Lightly dampen the pastry edges of the tartlets, and lay the remaining eight pastry rounds on top, removing any excess with a rolling pin. Chill in the refrigerator while you make the royal icing.

Royal icing

Beat the egg whites until standing in soft peaks, then fold in the powdered sugar using a spatula.

To assemble and finish

Using a spatula, spread a layer of royal icing over each tartlet.

Lay the pastry strips on top of the icing on each tartlet, interlacing them in a diamond pattern. Place the conversations on a baking sheet lined with parchment paper and leave to rest in the refrigerator for 30 minutes.

Preheat the oven to 350°F (180°C/Gas mark 4) and bake the conversations for 30 to 35 minutes.

This is one of the many recipes attributed to Antonin Carême in the 19th century. The story goes that the pastry chef of kings came up with the clever idea for the recipe when he saw Talleyrand dipping a sponge finger in a glass of Madeira to reduce the effect of the alcohol, a common practice at that time. He devised a recipe for a cookie (biscuit) that would not disintegrate when it was soaked. The name *boudoir* is believed to refer to the "boudoir diplomacy" the statesman conducted. The anecdote has survived, but the recipe may have been created much earlier by the pastry chef of Amédée VI of Savoy.

Boudoir biscuits

Preparation time: 25 minutes • Cooking time: 6 to 8 minutes

INGREDIENTS
TO MAKE ABOUT 20 BISCUITS

3½oz (100g) egg whites
½ cup (3½oz/100g) superfine (caster) sugar, plus extra for dusting
2½oz (75g) egg yolks
5½ tbsp (1¾oz/45g) all-purpose (plain) flour
½ cup less 1 tsp (1¾oz/45g) cornstarch (cornflour)

Preheat the oven to 425°F (210°C/Gas mark 7).

Whisk the egg whites in a bowl until they are standing in firm peaks. Whisk in the sugar in four or five batches (as for making meringue).

Using a spatula, mix some of the whisked egg whites with the egg yolks, making sure the two are evenly combined. Add the rest of the egg whites and fold in gently. Sift in the flour and cornstarch and fold in as well. Spoon the mixture into a piping bag fitted with a ½-inch (12-mm) plain tip. Line a baking sheet with parchment paper and pipe lines of the batter, 4 to 5 inches (10 to 12cm) long, spaced well apart. Sprinkle over a thin layer of superfine sugar twice and place immediately in the oven.

Bake for 6 to 8 minutes.

—

TIP:
YOU CAN REPLACE ⅔OZ (20G) SUGAR WITH ⅔OZ (20G) RUNNY HONEY (SUCH AS ACACIA HONEY) FOR A LONGER STORAGE TIME.

—

Baked Alaska
(Omelette Norvégienne)

Balzac, the chef at the Grand Hôtel on the boulevard des Capucines, created this dessert on the occasion of a dinner given for a Chinese delegation who had been invited by the City of Paris as part of the World Fair celebrations in 1867. At a time when the invention of electricity was the hot topic of the day, he came up with the perfect recipe using scientific experiments, carried out by the Earl of Rumford (an Anglo-American physicist who had emigrated to Bavaria), on the ability of beaten egg white to conduct heat. Balzac named his recipe *omelette Norvégienne* and while the French still love the ingenious idea of coating ice cream with meringue and baking it, they have forgiven the chef's geographical shortcomings in placing Bavaria in Norway.

•

Preparation time:
1 hour 30 minutes
Infusing time:
30 minutes
Cooking time:
20 minutes

•

EQUIPMENT

8½- or 9½-inch (22- or 24-cm) diameter mold, buttered and floured

INGREDIENTS TO SERVE 10

Vanilla ice cream 2¾ cups plus 2 tbsp (23fl oz/675ml) whole milk • ¾ cup plus 1½ tbsp (7fl oz/200ml) whipping cream (35% fat) • 1½ vanilla beans, slit lengthwise and seeds scraped out • 10 egg yolks • 1 cup (7oz/200g) superfine (caster) sugar

Genoese sponge 1 ⅓ cups (6¼oz/180g) all-purpose (plain) flour • 3½ tbsp (1¾oz/50g) butter • 10¼oz (290g) eggs (5 eggs) • 1 cup less 1½ tbsp (6¼oz/180g) superfine (caster) sugar

Syrup ½ cup plus 2 tbsp (5fl oz/150ml) water • ¾ cup (5½oz/150g) superfine (caster) sugar • 2 tsp (⅓fl oz/10ml) Grand Marnier

French meringue 4½oz (100g) egg whites • 1¼ cups (9oz/250g) superfine (caster) sugar

For finishing Powdered (icing) sugar • ¾ cup plus 1½ tbsp (7fl oz/200ml) Grand Marnier

Make the vanilla ice cream

You can make your own vanilla ice cream but, if you prefer, use an artisan-made one.

To make your own ice cream, bring the milk and cream to the boil in a saucepan. Add the vanilla beans and seeds, remove from the heat, cover, and leave to infuse for 30 minutes, then strain.

Vigorously whisk the egg yolks and sugar together in a mixing bowl. Pour in the infused milk, mix well, then pour the mixture back into the saucepan and cook it in the same way as for making a custard, until it coats the back of the spoon and the temperature reaches 180°F (82°C). Strain the custard through a fine sieve and leave it to cool in a water-bath to which ice cubes have been added. Churn in an ice-cream machine.

Make the Genoese sponge

Preheat the oven to 350°F (180°C/Gas mark 4).

Sift the flour and melt the butter.

Put the eggs and sugar in a mixing bowl. Stand the bowl over a simmering water-bath and whisk the eggs and sugar with an electric hand beater. When the temperature of the mixture reaches 131°F to 140°F (55°C to 60°C), increases in volume, and thickens (the bowl will feel hot to the touch but will be bearable), remove the bowl from the water-bath and continue whisking until the bowl is completely cold. Using a spatula, fold in the melted butter. Sift over the flour, a little at a time, folding in each addition before adding the next.

Pour the batter into the prepared mold. Bake for 20 minutes and leave to cool before turning out.

Make the syrup

Heat the water and sugar in a saucepan and bring to the boil once the sugar has dissolved. Leave to cool, then add the Grand Marnier.

Start to assemble

Cut the sponge horizontally into two rounds and brush them with the Grand Marnier syrup. Top the first round with vanilla ice cream and cover it with the second round. Store in the freezer while you make the meringue.

Make the French meringue

Whisk the egg whites until standing in firm peaks and then gradually whisk in the sugar, a little at a time, until the whites are stiff.

To finish

Remove the ice cream-filled Genoese sponge from the freezer. Using a flexible spatula, cover the Genoese with meringue. You can decorate it by piping the meringue in swirls using a fluted icing tip. Dust with powdered sugar and broil (grill) for 1 to 2 minutes, using the oven broiler (grill) or a chef's blowtorch, to lightly brown the meringue. At the last moment, heat the Grand Marnier in a small saucepan. Set it alight and pour it over the Baked Alaska. Present it to your guests at the table before the flames die down.

In 1815, Antonin Carême wrote a recipe in his *Pâtissier royal parisien* (*The Royal Parisian Pastry Chef*) cookery book for a *croque-en-bouche*, which appeared again in Bailleux's *Pâtissier royal* (*Royal Pastry Chef*) with the one-word spelling it has today. Carême created the recipe for these small, caramelized choux buns that are stacked to form magnificent *pièces montées*. It is said that he first served this dessert at Prince Berthier's table.

Croquembouche

Preparation time:
2 hours
Cooking time:
20 to 25 minutes

INGREDIENTS TO SERVE 6 TO 8

Crème pâtissière ¾ cup plus 1½ tbsp (7fl oz/200ml) whole milk • 1 vanilla bean, slit lengthwise and seeds scraped out • ½ egg yolk • 5 tbsp (2oz/60g) superfine (caster) sugar • ½ oz (15g) custard powder

Choux pastry 3½ tbsp (1¾fl oz/50ml) whole milk • 3½ tbsp (1¾fl oz/50ml) water • ½ tsp (2g) salt • ½ tsp (2g) superfine (caster) sugar • 3 tbsp (1¾oz/45g) butter, cut into small pieces • 4¼ tbsp (1¼oz/35g) all-purpose (plain) flour • 3½oz (100g) eggs • Melted butter for the baking sheet

Nougatine 3½oz (100g) chopped almonds • ½ cup (4½oz/100g) superfine (caster) sugar • ¼ cup (2fl oz/60ml) water • ¼ cup (2¼oz/65g) liquid glucose

Boiled sugar 2½ tbsp (1½fl oz/40ml) water • ⅔ cup (4¾oz/130g) superfine (caster) sugar • 2 tsp (⅓fl oz/10ml) liquid glucose

For decoration A few sugared almonds

Make the crème pâtissière

Heat the milk, vanilla bean, and seeds in a saucepan over a medium heat. Whisk the egg yolk with the sugar in a mixing bowl. Pour a little of the hot milk over, stir to mix, then pour this mixture back into the saucepan. Add the custard powder and cook, stirring frequently, until it is thickened and smooth. Press plastic wrap (cling film) over the surface and leave to cool, before chilling in the refrigerator.

Make the choux pastry

Preheat the oven to 425°F (210°C/Gas mark 7). Brush a baking sheet with melted butter.

Bring the milk, water, salt, sugar, and butter to the boil in a saucepan over a low heat. Remove the pan from the heat and add all the flour in one go, then mix briskly with a spatula until you have a smooth, soft dough. Return the pan to the heat and dry out the dough for around 10 seconds. Scrape it into a mixing bowl (to stop the cooking). Using a spatula, gradually beat in the eggs, checking the consistency as you go. If you trace a groove in the dough, it should close up slowly.

Spoon the dough into a piping bag fitted with a ½-inch (12-mm) plain tip and pipe 30 buns about 1¼ inches (3cm) in diameter onto the buttered baking sheet, spacing them well apart. Bake for

Recipe continues on next page

20 to 25 minutes without opening the oven door during the first 20 minutes of cooking or you risk the buns collapsing.

Make the nougatine

Line a baking sheet with parchment paper and spread the almonds over it. Roast them under the oven broiler (grill) or in the oven preheated to 325°F (160°C/Gas mark 3).

Heat the sugar and water in a saucepan over a medium heat and, once the sugar has dissolved, bring to the boil. Add the liquid glucose and boil until the syrup is caramel colored.

Stir in the roasted almonds. Lightly oil a marble or stainless steel (heat-resistant) surface and pour the almond mixture onto it. Spread it in an even layer with a rolling pin. When firm enough, cut out a 5½-inch (14-cm) disk and cut the remainder into triangles or other shapes.

Make the boiled sugar

Heat the water and sugar in a saucepan over a medium heat and bring to the boil. Once boiling, add the liquid glucose and cook until the temperature reaches 262°F (128°C). Stop the cooking by plunging the base of the saucepan into a bowl of cold water.

To assemble

Spoon the crème pâtissière into a piping bag fitted with a ½-inch (12-mm) plain tip. Pierce a small hole in the bottom of each choux bun and fill the buns with the crème pâtissière. Glaze the buns by dipping them in the boiled sugar so half of each bun is coated, taking care not to burn yourself. Stick a row of dipped buns on the nougatine disk, then add a second row of buns on top of these. Continue in the same way, decreasing the number of buns at each level to create a beautiful conical shape. Decorate with the nougatine triangles, dipping in the boiled sugar to "glue" them in place. Add a few sugared almonds for decoration.

With the suffix *"ette"* suggesting their diminutive size, *chouquettes* are reputed to have been created by Popelini, a fictional pastry chef under Catherine de Medici in the 16th century. It is said he developed a recipe based on pastry dried over a fire and called *popelini*, *popelin*, or *poupelin*. This "hot pastry" is a forerunner of the choux pastry that Jean Avice (Talleyrand's pastry chef) perfected, followed by Antonin Carême. Many choux pastry recipes, in addition to chouquettes that are sprinkled with pearl sugar, were created from this classic dough.

Chouquettes

Preparation time:
30 minutes
Cooking time:
20 to 25 minutes

INGREDIENTS TO MAKE ABOUT 50 CHOUQUETTES

- 1 cup (9fl oz/250ml) water (or ½ cup/4½fl oz/125ml whole milk and ½ cup/4½fl oz/125ml water)
- ½ tsp (2.5g) salt
- ½ tsp (2.5g) superfine (caster) sugar
- 7 tbsp (3½oz/100g) butter
- 1 cup plus 2 tbsp (5½oz/150g) all-purpose (plain) flour
- 7½oz (210g) eggs
- 1 tsp (⅛oz/5g) liquid vanilla flavoring (optional)
- Pearl sugar, to decorate

Preheat the oven to 425°F (210°C/Gas mark 7). Line a baking sheet with parchment paper.

Bring the water (or milk and water), salt, sugar, and butter to the boil in a saucepan. Take the pan off the heat and add all the flour in one go, then mix briskly with a spatula until you have a smooth, soft dough. Return the pan to the heat and dry out the dough for around 10 seconds. Scrape it into a mixing bowl (to stop the cooking). Using a spatula, gradually beat in the eggs, checking the consistency as you go. If you trace a groove in the dough, it should close up slowly. Add the vanilla flavoring, if using.

Spoon the dough into a piping bag fitted with a ⅝-inch (15-mm) plain tip and pipe choux buns on the baking sheet, 1¼ to 1½ inches (3 to 4cm) in diameter and about 1¼ inches (3cm) apart.

Sprinkle each bun with pearl sugar, removing any sugar than falls onto the baking sheet, and bake for 20 to 25 minutes. Do not open the oven door during cooking or you risk the buns collapsing.

VARIATION:
YOU CAN SPRINKLE THE CHOUQUETTES WITH CHOCOLATE CHIPS IF YOU PREFER.

VILLON MOLLIEN

This little-known gâteau, a cousin of the friand, only became known in the 1770s when it was sold at the Flon pâtisserie in the rue Saint-Germain-l'Auxerrois.

Marcelin

•

Preparation time:
30 minutes
Cooking time:
30 minutes

•

EQUIPMENT

7-inch (18-cm) round cake pan, 1½ inches (4cm) high

INGREDIENTS TO SERVE 8

12oz (350g) sweet tart pastry (see page 131) • 4¼oz (120g) candied fruits, chopped • ½ cup (1¾oz/50g) ground almonds • 5¾ tbsp (1¾oz/50g) powdered (icing) sugar, plus extra for dusting • 2oz (60g) egg yolks • 1½oz (40g) beaten egg • 3 tbsp (1oz/25g) all-purpose (plain) flour • ¼ cup plus 1 tbsp (1oz/25g) rice flour • 1 tbsp plus 2 tsp (25g) butter • Seeds from ½ vanilla bean • 2 tsp (⅓oz/10g) Grand Marnier • 1¾oz (45g) egg whites • 2½ tbsp (1oz/30g) superfine (caster) sugar • Flaked almonds • Butter for the pan

Make the sweet tart pastry and roll it out ⅛ inch (3mm) thick. Cut out a disc about 14 inches (36cm) in diameter. Butter the cake pan and line it with the pastry. Spread the chopped candied fruits over the pastry base. Keep refrigerated until needed.

Preheat the oven to 350°F (180°C/Gas mark 4).

Fit a stand mixer with the flat beater attachment and beat together the ground almonds, powdered sugar, egg yolks, and whole egg, adding the latter a little at a time. Sift in the flours and mix in. Melt the butter in a saucepan or microwave and add the vanilla seeds. Add the warm vanilla butter to the almond batter, followed by the Grand Marnier.

Whisk the egg whites in a bowl using an electric hand beater, then whisk in the superfine sugar until the whites are stiff. Carefully fold the whites into the batter using a spatula.

Remove the chilled pastry case from the refrigerator and spoon the batter into it. Sprinkle over flaked almonds and dust with powdered sugar. Bake for about 30 minutes. Check the tart is cooked by pushing the tip of a pointed knife into the center; it is cooked if the knife comes out dry.

Leave to cool before turning out.

In 1839, in the service of James Mayer de Rothschild, Antonin Carême created a sweet soufflé with a pastry cream base. He perfected and built upon recipes created in the second half of the 18th century by a number of chefs, including Massialot, Viard and Beauvilliers. Acknowledged by Alexandre Dumas in his *Grand Dictionnaire de cuisine* (1873) and in the movie *Le Grand Restaurant* (1966) by Louis de Funès, his fame remains undimmed.

Soufflé

Preparation time:
45 minutes
Cooking time:
20 to 25 minutes

EQUIPMENT

8 ramekins 3½ inches (9cm) in diameter and 1¾ inches (4.5cm) high or a 7½-inch (19-cm) soufflé dish 3½ inches (9cm) high

INGREDIENTS TO SERVE 10

Crème pâtissière 1¾ cups (14fl oz/400ml) whole milk • 6½ tbsp (2¾oz/80g) superfine (caster) sugar • ½ vanilla bean, slit lengthwise and seeds scraped out • 2¾oz (80g) eggs • ¼ cup (¾oz/20g) cornstarch (cornflour) • 2⅓ tbsp (¾oz/20g) all-purpose (plain) flour • 3 tbsp (1½oz/40g) butter, cut into small pieces • 1 tbsp plus 1 tsp (20ml) absinthe or Grand Marnier

Soufflé 10½oz (300g) egg whites • ¾ cup less ½ tbsp (3½oz/100g) powdered (icing) sugar • Melted butter and superfine (caster) sugar for greasing and dusting the ramekins

Make the crème pâtissière

Heat the milk in a saucepan with half the sugar and the vanilla bean and seeds.

In a mixing bowl, whisk the eggs with the rest of the sugar until pale and thickened. Sift in the cornstarch and flour and fold in.

When the milk mixture comes to the boil, remove the vanilla pod. Pour some of the vanilla-flavored milk onto the egg mixture to loosen it, mix it in, then pour it back into the saucepan. Stir well until the two mixtures are combined, then bring to the boil and cook for 2 to 3 minutes.

Take the pan off the heat and mix in the butter. Transfer the crème pâtissière to a bowl, press plastic wrap (cling film) over the surface and leave to cool.

Make the soufflé

Preheat the oven to 400°F (200°C/Gas mark 6).

Brush the ramekins or the soufflé dish lightly with melted butter and dust with superfine sugar.

Return the crème pâtissière to a saucepan and whisk over the heat until lukewarm and the temperature reaches 95°F to 104°F (35°C to 40°C). Add your chosen alcohol.

Whisk the egg whites to firm peaks, then carefully fold in the crème pâtissière using a flexible spatula.

Fill the ramekins with the mixture, smooth the tops, and dust with powdered sugar. Run your finger around the top edge of each ramekin to remove any excess mixture. Bake in the oven for 20 to 25 minutes and serve at once.

These little éclairs are a variation on a recipe as old as choux pastry that was perfected by Antonin Carême in the 19th century. The master pastry chef, whose store was on the rue Jean-Jacques Rousseau, is said to have named these delicacies "Caroline" after a dancer he was wooing.

•

Preparation time:
1 hour
Chilling time:
30 minutes
Cooking time:
30 minutes

•

Carolines

INGREDIENTS
TO MAKE 30 CAROLINES

Choux pastry

- 2/3 cup (3¼oz/90g) all-purpose (plain) flour
- 5 tbsp (2½fl oz/75ml) whole milk
- 5 tbsp (2½fl oz/75ml) water
- ½ tsp (2.5g) salt
- ½ tsp (2.5g) superfine (caster) sugar
- ¼ cup (2oz/60g) butter, cut into small pieces, plus optional extra for greasing
- 5½oz (150g) beaten egg

Make the choux pastry

Preheat the oven to 350°F (180°C/Gas mark 4). Grease a baking sheet with butter (or line it with parchment paper).Sift the flour.

Bring the milk, water, salt, sugar, and butter to the boil in a saucepan.When boiling, remove the pan from the heat, add all the flour in one go and mix in with a spatula. Lightly dry the mixture over the heat; the dough needs to form into a ball in the center of the saucepan. Transfer the dough to a bowl and beat in the eggs, a little at a time, using a spatula. The dough must have a soft, supple consistency.

Transfer the dough to a piping bag fitted with a ½-inch (12-mm) plain tip and pipe mini-éclairs onto the prepared baking sheet, 2 inches (5cm) long and about ⅝ inch (1.5cm) wide, spacing them 1¼ to 1½ inches (3 to 4cm) apart.

Bake for 30 minutes. Avoid opening the oven door for the first 20 minutes cooking time as the choux risks collapsing. During the last 5 minutes, prop the oven door open with a wooden spatula to dry out the choux or open the oven door three or four times to let the steam escape.

Recipe continues on next page

Chocolate cream

½ cup (4fl oz/120ml) whipping cream (35% fat)
½ cup (4fl oz/120ml) whole milk
1¾oz (50g) egg yolks
2 tbsp (1oz/25g) superfine (caster) sugar
3½oz (100g) bittersweet (dark) chocolate (70% cacao), chopped

Chocolate icing

1 tbsp plus 1 tsp (20ml) water
1 tbsp plus 2 tsp (¾oz/20g) sugar
3 tbsp (¾oz/20g) unsweetened cocoa powder
9oz (250g) fondant icing

Make the chocolate cream

Bring the cream and milk to the boil in a saucepan. Whisk the egg yolks and sugar together in a mixing bowl until pale and thickened, then pour on the milk and cream a little at a time, whisking constantly. Return the mixture to the saucepan and cook until it coats the back of a spoon and the temperature reaches 180°F to 183°F (82°C to 84°C). Put the chopped chocolate in a bowl and strain the cream mixture through a fine sieve onto the chocolate. Using an upright blender, mix everything together until smooth, keeping the beater arm immersed so as not to introduce any air. Chill in the refrigerator for 30 minutes.

Make the chocolate icing

Heat the water and sugar in a microwave to make a syrup. Once the sugar has dissolved, add the cocoa powder and whisk in. Heat the fondant in a saucepan to 95°F to 104°F (35°C to 40°C). Add the chocolate syrup to give a chocolate color and make a fondant that is softer to work with.

To assemble

Using a skewer, pierce two or three small holes in the base of each éclair. Spoon the chocolate cream into a piping bag fitted with a ¼-inch (6-mm) tip and fill the éclairs with the cream. Pick up each Caroline and dip the top in the chocolate icing. Smooth the edges of the icing neatly with your finger. Chill the éclairs until ready to serve.

1er Arr.
PLACE
VENDÔME

This cake, aptly named the "Three Brothers' Cake" (*Gateau des Trois-Frères*) was created by Arthur, Auguste, and Narcisse Julien, who were renowned pastry chefs in the place de la Bourse. The brothers were responsible for developing many classic recipes that have survived the centuries, including the Moka, Savarin, Talleyrand, and Richelieu. Created in 1851, the "Three Brothers' Cake" or simply "Three Brothers" was baked in a cake pan specially designed for it by Trottier Paris, who made copper cake pans, and who patented it in 1857.

Three brothers' cake

Preparation time:
30 minutes
Cooking time:
25 to 30 minutes

EQUIPMENT

7-inch (18-cm) round cake pan (a three brothers' pan, if possible)

INGREDIENTS
TO SERVE 6

- ½ cup less ¼ tbsp (3¾oz/110g) butter
- ½ vanilla bean, slit lengthwise and seeds scraped out
- ¾ cup (5½oz/150g) superfine (caster) sugar
- 8½oz (240g) eggs
- ¾ cup (3¾oz/110g) rice flour
- Butter and flour for the cake pan

NOTE:
ORIGINALLY THE CAKE WAS DECORATED WITH A LAYER OF APRICOT LIQUEUR AND APRICOT JAM, PLUS PRALINES AND ANGELICA.

Preheat the oven to 350°F (180°C/Gas mark 4). Butter and flour the cake pan.

Melt the butter in a saucepan with the half vanilla bean and the seeds. Remove the bean and set aside.

In a stainless steel bowl, beat the sugar and eggs together over the heat. This can be done in a water-bath or directly on the hob, but you must not let the bowl get so hot you cannot touch the bottom of it with your hand.

Once the mixture is light colored and airy, use a flexible spatula to fold in the rice flour, followed by the melted vanilla butter.

Pour the batter into the prepared cake pan. Bake for 25 to 30 minutes.

VALENTINO
VALENTINO
VALENTINO
PATEK PHILIPPE
PATEK PHILIPPE
PATEK PHILIPPE
MIKIMOTO
MIKIMOTO
MIKIMOTO
MIKIMOTO
8

VALENTINO
VALENTINO
VALENTINO
VALENTINO
DIOR
DIOR
REPOSSI
REPOSSI
6

A savory version of this dish from medieval times was very popular in the 17th century. For a long time, a blancmange was eaten both as a main course and a dessert but, in the 19th century, Antonin Carême transformed it into a striking dessert with whipped cream and flavored with, among other things, rum, vanilla, and citron. By the beginning of the following century, Auguste Ecoffier was lamenting that blancmange was rarely prepared, despite it being "one of the finest entremets that can be served, when well made."

Blancmange

Preparation time:
1 hour 30 minutes
Freezing time:
2 to 3 hours
Cooking time:
12 to 15 minutes

EQUIPMENT

8½-inch (22-cm) round baking ring

INGREDIENTS TO SERVE 8

Almond dacquoise 3oz (85g) egg whites · 1 tbsp plus 2 tsp (¾oz/20g) superfine (caster) sugar · 2¼ tbsp (¾oz/20g) powdered (icing) sugar · 1¾ tbsp (½oz/15g) all-purpose (plain) flour · Scant ½ cup (1¾oz/45g) ground almonds

Almond milk mousse 2 cups (17fl oz/500ml) whipping cream (35% fat) · ¼oz (7g) powdered gelatin · 3 tbsp (1½oz/42ml) cold water · ½ cup (4½fl oz/125ml) almond milk · ½ tsp liquid vanilla flavoring · 4¼oz (120g) pineapple canned in syrup, drained

To assemble and decorate 2oz (60g) raspberries, plus a few extra for decoration · 3½oz (100g) apricot glaze or neutral glaze

Make the almond dacquoise

Preheat the oven to 325°F (160°C/Gas mark 3). Line a baking sheet with parchment paper.

Whisk the egg whites in a mixing bowl until standing in firm peaks, then whisk in the superfine sugar in two or three batches.

Sift the powdered sugar, the flour, and the ground almonds. Once the egg whites are beaten, add the sifted ingredients and fold in with a flexible spatula. Pour the batter onto the lined baking sheet it, and spread it in a round 8½ inches (22cm) in diameter. Bake for 12 to 15 minutes.

When the dacquoise comes out of the oven, slide it onto a wire rack.

Make the almond milk mousse

Whip the cream and chill it in the refrigerator until needed. Soak the gelatin in the water to rehydrate it. In a saucepan, warm the almond milk, add the vanilla, and then the gelatin, whisking the ingredients together to dissolve the gelatin. Add the almond milk mixture to the cream and stir the two together. Cut the pineapple into small pieces and mix in.

To assemble and decorate

Cover a large plate with plastic wrap (cling film) and place the baking ring on top. Halve the raspberries and arrange them in the middle of the ring. Fill the ring with almond milk mousse and lay the dacquoise on top. Freeze for 2 to 3 hours.

Heat the glaze in a saucepan or microwave. Remove the blancmange from the freezer, turn it upside down onto a serving plate and remove the ring and plastic wrap. Brush with the glaze and decorate with a few extra raspberries.

Antonin Carême is said to have created this recipe at the request of Talleyrand, who wanted something that could be eaten and enjoyed by everyone without needing to be reheated during the diplomat's lengthy negotiations at the Congress of Vienna in 1815. The so-called "king of chefs and chef of kings" made himself indispensable to the politician, who regarded Carême's cooking as a highly strategic weapon in his negotiating arsenal.

Diplomat

with glacé fruits

•

Preparation time:
35 minutes
Cooking time:
1 hour

•

EQUIPMENT

8½-inch (22-cm) charlotte mold

INGREDIENTS
TO SERVE 6 TO 8

7oz (200g) glacé fruits
7 tbsp (3½fl oz/100ml) sugarcane juice rum
Heaped ½ cup (2¾oz/80g) raisins
1lb 2oz (500g) brioche loaf
3 tbsp (1½oz/40g) butter
1 cup (7oz/200g) superfine (caster) sugar
½ tsp liquid vanilla flavoring or 1oz (30g) vanilla sugar
1 cup (9fl oz/250ml) whole milk
6 eggs
Butter and sugar for the mold

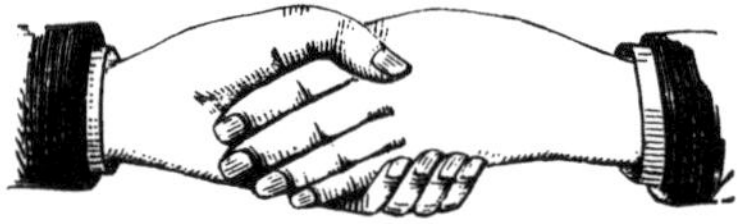

Chop the glacé fruits and leave them to macerate in the rum with the raisins.

Preheat the oven to 300°F (150°C/Gas mark 2).

Cut the brioche loaf into slices about ¾ inch (2cm) thick. Trim the edges (retaining the crust). Melt the butter and brush it over both sides of the brioche slices. Toast the slices lightly on each side under the broiler (grill).

Drain the raisins and glacé fruits, reserving the rum. Butter the charlotte mold and dust it with sugar. Line the bottom of the mold with toasted brioche slices and sprinkle with some of the raisins and glacé fruits. Cover with a layer of brioche slices and then raisins and glacé fruits. Repeat the layers until the mold is full.

In a mixing bowl, whisk together the sugar, vanilla flavoring or vanilla sugar, milk, eggs, and the reserved rum. Pour this mixture a little at a time into the charlotte mold so the brioche has time to absorb it.

Bake for 1 hour in a water-bath, making sugar the mixture does not boil. Leave to cool before removing from the mold. Serve chilled.

Chiboust tart

•
Preparation time:
1 hour 35 minutes
Chilling time:
2 hours
Freezing time:
2 hours
Cooking time:
20 minutes
•

EQUIPMENT

8½-inch (22-cm) tart ring

INGREDIENTS TO SERVE 8

(9oz/250g) sweet tart pastry (see page 131) · Brown sugar, for sprinkling

Almond cream ¼ cup (2oz/60g) softened butter · 5 tbsp (2oz/60g) superfine (caster) sugar · ⅔ cup (2oz/60g) ground almonds · 2oz (60g) eggs, beaten · 3½ tsp (⅓oz/10g) all-purpose (plain) flour · 1 tsp sugarcane juice rum · Seeds from ½ vanilla bean

Pan-fried apples 1lb 2oz (500g) apples · 3 tbsp (1½oz/40g) butter · 5 tbsp (2oz/60g) superfine (caster) sugar

Crème pâtissière ¾ cup plus 1½ tbsp (7fl oz/200ml) whole milk · ½ cup plus 1½ tbsp (4½fl oz/140ml) whipping cream (35% fat) · 2oz (60g) egg yolks · 6 tbsp (2½oz/75g) superfine (caster) sugar · 2 tbsp (⅔oz/18g) all-purpose (plain) flour · 1 tbsp (¼ oz/8g) cornstarch (cornflour) · ⅛oz (5g) powdered gelatin · 2 tbsp water · ⅔ cup (5½oz/150g) mascarpone · 1 tsp natural vanilla flavoring

Italian meringue 4½oz (100g) egg whites · ½ cup (4½oz/100g) superfine (caster) sugar · 2 tbsp plus 2 tsp (1½fl oz/40ml) water

Prepare the sweet tart pastry. Roll out ¹⁄₁₀ inch (2.5mm) thick to a disc 12 inches (30cm) in diameter. Place the tart ring on a baking sheet, line the pastry into it, and trim. Refrigerate.

Make the almond cream

While the pastry is resting, make the almond cream. Fit a stand mixer with the flat beater attachment and beat the butter and sugar together on low speed. Add the ground almonds and then the eggs a little at a time. Continue beating until the mixture is smooth, using a pastry scraper or flexible spatula to scrape down the sides of the bowl, if necessary. Next add the flour, rum, and vanilla seeds. Set aside at room temperature.

Preheat the oven to 350°F (180°C/Gas mark 4).

Cook the apples

Peel, core, and cut each apple into eight. Melt the butter and sugar in a frying pan and fry the apple wedges over a brisk heat for 5 minutes. Fill the tart case with the almond cream, spread out the apple pieces on top and bake for 20 to 25 minutes.

Make the crème pâtissière

Bring the milk and cream to the boil in a saucepan. Whisk the egg yolks and sugar in a mixing bowl until pale and thick, then sift in the flour and cornstarch. Add some of the hot milk and cream, stir well, and then return the mixture to the saucepan. Stir constantly over the heat until thickened and smooth and leave to boil for 2 to 3 minutes. Rehydrate the gelatin in the water, then stir this into the hot crème pâtissière, mixing with a whisk. Finally, add the mascarpone and vanilla flavoring. Mix again and leave the crème pâtissière to keep warm in the saucepan.

Make the Italian meringue

Fit a stand mixer with the whisk attachment and whisk the egg whites until standing in firm peaks. Dissolve the sugar in the water in a saucepan and boil until the temperature of the syrup reaches 248°F (120°C). Pour the syrup in a thin, steady stream into the beaten egg whites, whisking constantly. Once all the syrup has been incorporated, continue whisking for 1 to 2 minutes. In a mixing bowl, gently whisk together the Italian meringue and the crème pâtissière. Spread this Chiboust cream over the tart. Freeze for 2 hours. Once the Chiboust cream is set, dust it with brown sugar and caramelize the tart using a chef's blowtorch, repeating this twice or three times as you wish. Chill until ready to serve but, be aware, that the humidity in a refrigerator tends to soften caramel, so caramelize the tart just before serving.

Preparation time:
30 minutes
Cooking time:
35 to 40 minutes

EQUIPMENT

8-inch (20-cm) round cake pan

INGREDIENTS
TO SERVE 6

6¼oz (180g) marzipan, chopped
1¾oz (50g) egg yolks
6¼oz (180g) whole eggs
½ tsp liquid vanilla flavoring
⅓ cup (1¼oz/35g) cornstarch (cornflour)
¾ tsp (3g) baking powder
¼ cup (2oz/60g) butter, melted
1¼oz (35g) flaked almonds
Butter and flour for the cake pan

In the 1850s, Fauvel, who was a pastry chef at Maison Chiboust (which, at that time, was a breeding ground for chefs with creative ideas), developed a modern version of this Genoese sponge, also known as *Ambroisie*. When he left the rue Saint-Honoré store to move to Maison Frascati on the boulevard Montmartre, he took his recipe with him and renamed it Genoese bread.

Genoese bread

Preheat the oven to 400°F (200°C/Gas mark 6). Butter and flour the cake pan.

Soften the marzipan in a microwave for a few seconds, if necessary.

Fit a stand mixer with the flat beater attachment and beat the softened marzipan with the egg yolks on medium speed until combined. Add the whole eggs, followed by the vanilla flavoring. Change the flat beater attachment for the whisk and, still on medium speed, beat for about 10 minutes. Sift in the cornstarch and baking powder and fold them into the marzipan and egg mixture using a spatula. Gradually incorporate the melted butter, mixing it in gently.

Sprinkle the flaked almonds evenly over the base of the cake pan, then pour the batter into the pan and place in the oven. Immediately lower the oven temperature to 350°F (180°C/Gas mark 4) and bake for 35 to 40 minutes.

When the cake is cooked, turn it out onto a wire rack and leave to cool.

The "*gâteau manqué*" was dubbed a failure because a young pastry chef working at Maison Félix in 1842 managed to turn one of his errors into a classic recipe. Overwhelmed by the need to prepare Savoy sponges in a hurry, the owner—or his apprentice, depending on who you believe—tried to correct the mistake by adding butter and a layer of praline, much to the delight of the customer who had placed the order.

"Failure" cake

Preparation time:
20 minutes
Cooking time:
20 minutes

EQUIPMENT

8½-inch (22-cm) round cake pan

INGREDIENTS
TO SERVE 8

- 1 cup plus 2 tbsp (5½/150g) all-purpose (plain) flour
- 7 tbsp (3½oz/105g) butter
- Seeds from 1 vanilla bean
- 10½oz (300g) eggs (about 6 eggs)
- 1 cup plus 1½ tbsp (7¾oz/220g) superfine (caster) sugar
- 1½ tbsp (¾oz/22ml) sugarcane juice rum
- 1 pinch of salt
- Butter and flour for the cake pan

Preheat the oven to 350°F (180°C/Gas mark 4). Butter and flour the cake pan.

Sift the flour.

In a saucepan, melt the butter with the vanilla seeds over a medium heat. Set aside to infuse.

Separate the egg whites from the yolks.

Whisk the egg whites with the sugar in a mixing bowl until pale and thickened: the mixture must be mousse-like. Sift the flour again over the surface, then fold in with the vanilla butter and rum, using a spatula, until the batter is smooth. Whisk the egg whites with the salt and, using a flexible spatula, fold them gently into the batter.

Transfer the batter to the prepared pan and bake for 20 minutes.

When the cake comes out of the oven, turn it out onto a wire rack to cool.

NOTE:
IF YOU WISH YOU CAN ADD RAISINS, ANISEEDS, OR CHOPPED NUTS SUCH AS HAZELNUTS AND ALMONDS, TO THE BATTER.

Rum babas

•

Preparation time: 30 minutes
Resting time:
15 minutes + 24 hours
Rising time: 1–2 hours
Cooking time: 15 minutes

•

EQUIPMENT

8 baba molds

INGREDIENTS FOR 8 RUM BABAS

Babas (prepare the day before)

½ cup less 1 tbsp (3½oz/100g) butter
1¾ cups plus 2 tbsp (9oz/250g) all-purpose (plain) flour
Finely grated zest of ½ lemon
1½ tbsp (1oz/25g) acacia honey
2 tsp (⅛oz/8g) salt
¾oz (20g) baker's (fresh) yeast
1lb (450g) eggs (about 8 eggs)
Butter for the molds

Syrup

4¼ cups (35fl oz/1 litre) water
Finely grated zest of ½ orange
Seeds from 1 vanilla bean
1½ cups (10½oz/300g) superfine (caster) sugar
7 tbsp (3½fl oz/100ml) sugarcane juice rum

To finish and for decoration

Scant ½ cup (3½oz/100g) apricot glaze
Scant ½ to generous ¾ cup (3½fl oz to 7fl oz/100 to 200ml) sugarcane juice rum
8 glacé cherries
8 small pieces of angelica

Make the babas the day before

Cut the butter into small cubes and leave to come to room temperature.

Fit a stand mixer with the dough hook attachment and put the flour, lemon zest, honey, salt, yeast, and four of the eggs in the bowl, taking care to make sure the yeast does not come into contact with the salt and sugar.

Mix on medium speed until you have a dough that comes away from the sides of the bowl. Add the four remaining eggs and knead again. When the dough once again comes away from the sides of the bowl, add the cubed butter. Knead again and when you have a smooth, very supple dough, transfer it to a large mixing bowl and leave it to rest for 15 minutes at room temperature.

Butter the baba molds. Transfer the dough to a piping bag fitted with a large plain tip and pipe the dough into the molds until they are half full. Leave to rise at room temperature until the dough rises to the tops of the molds. Preheat the oven to 400°F (200°C/Gas mark 6) and bake the babas for 15 minutes. Leave to cool in the molds before turning them out onto a wire rack. It is preferable to prepare the babas 24 hours ahead as they will absorb the syrup better when they are dry.

Make the syrup

Bring the water, orange zest, vanilla seeds, and sugar to the boil in a saucepan. Take the pan off the heat and add the rum. Soak the babas, one by one, for 1 minute each in the hot syrup.

To finish and decorate

Bring the apricot glaze to the boil in a saucepan. Drench the babas with the rum, then brush them with the apricot glaze. Decorate with glacé cherries and small pieces of angelica.

Originally made from brioche dough and flavored with raisins and saffron, the baba was a 16th century Polish specialty. Based on the *kougelhof*, 200 years later King Stanislas Leszczynski took the recipe with him from Poland when he was exiled to Lorraine. It is said the monarch asked pastry chef Nicolas Stohrer to soak it to give it a softer texture. The Lunéville pastry chef then moved to Paris, opening a store on rue de Montorgueil, where he started a rum baba craze in the 1730s. To add to the legend, whether served as individual babas or as a large one to share, the baba is said to be a tribute to Ali Baba, a character from the Polish monarch's favorite fairy tale.

PATISSIER STOHRER
CHOCOLAT
PATISSIER

The talented and astute Auguste Julien perfected this recipe in his family's pâtisserie in the place de la Bourse, around 1845. It's the baba's twin brother, made with leavened dough and with candied orange zest replacing the raisins. Shaped like a crown, it owes its name to that colossus of French gastronomy, Jean Anthelme Brillat-Savarin.

Savarin

Preparation time: 30 minutes
Rising time: 45 minutes
Cooking time: 15 to 20 minutes

EQUIPMENT

10 savarin molds

INGREDIENTS FOR 10 SAVARINS

Baba dough 1¾ cups plus 2 tbsp (9oz/250g) all-purpose (plain) flour · 1½ tsp (⅛oz/6g) salt · 1½ tsp (⅛oz/6g) superfine (caster) sugar · ⅓oz (10g) baker's (fresh) yeast · 7 tbsp (3½fl oz/100ml) whole milk · 5¾oz (165g) eggs · 5 tbsp (2½oz/75g) tempered butter · 3½ tbsp (1¾oz/50g) butter, diced · Butter for the molds

Syrup 3 cups (24fl oz700ml) water · 1¾ cups (12oz/350g) superfine (caster) sugar · 1 vanilla bean (optional), slit lengthwise and seeds scraped out · 7 tbsp (3½fl oz/100ml) sugarcane juice rum (optional)

To finish and for decoration Scant ½ cup (3½oz/100g) neutral patisserie glaze or apricot glaze · 1¼ cups (10½fl oz/300ml) whipping cream (35% fat) · 6¾ tbsp (2oz/60g) powdered (icing) sugar · 2 tsp (⅓oz/10g) vanilla sugar

Make the baba dough

Fit a stand mixer with the flat beater attachment and put the flour, salt, sugar, yeast, and milk in the bowl, taking care to make sure the yeast does not come into contact with the salt and sugar. Mix on very low speed, then add the eggs in two equal batches and knead on medium speed for 6 to 8 minutes until the dough is smooth and elastic. Add the butters. The dough should be smooth and able to be stretched easily between your fingers without it tearing. Cover the dough with a dish towel and leave it to rest for 15 minutes at room temperature.

Butter the savarin molds. Knock down the baba dough and divide it into ten pieces (each about 1oz/25g). Press each piece of dough into a mold. The dough will be slightly sticky but this is normal so do not add extra flour. Leave the savarins to rise for 30 minutes at room temperature.

Preheat the oven to 400°F (200°C/Gas mark 6) and bake the savarins for 15 minutes. When they come out of the oven, turn the savarins out of their molds and leave them to cool on a wire rack.

While the savarins are baking, prepare the syrup.

Make the syrup

Heat the water and sugar in a saucepan over a high heat to make a syrup. You can add the vanilla bean and seeds now or with the rum at the end of cooking.

Soak the savarins in the hot syrup, making sure they are soaked right to the center. Leave them to drain on a wire rack.

To finish and decorate

Heat the glaze in a saucepan and brush it over the savarins. Place them in paper cases, if wished.

Whip the cream with the powdered sugar and the vanilla sugar. Spoon the cream into a piping bag fitted with a ½-inch (12-mm) serrated tip and pipe beautiful rosettes of cream inside each savarin.

Keep in the refrigerator until ready to serve.

accepte plus les chèques,
Ticket Restaurant
chèque déjeuner

Created in 1846 at the renowned Chiboust pâtisserie on the rue Saint-Honoré, this emblematic gâteau is named after the patron saint of pastry chefs. The expert hands of the Julien brothers and Chiboust perfected both the base and the cream filling of the iconic recipe. At that time, the Saint-Honoré was a brioche crown decorated with brioche buns and filled with crème pâtissière. The puff pastry version that had less cream was crafted by the same hands but came later.

Preparation time:
1 hour 30 minutes
Chilling time:
1 hour
Cooking time:
30 minutes

Saint-Honoré

INGREDIENTS
TO SERVE 8

Saint-Honoré cream

- ⅔ cup (5¼fl oz/160ml) whole milk
- Scant ½ cup (3¾fl oz/115ml) whipping cream (35% fat)
- ½ vanilla bean, slit lengthwise and seeds scraped out
- 1¾oz (50g) egg yolks
- 5 tbsp (2oz/60g) superfine (caster) sugar
- 1 tbsp (6g) cornstarch (cornflour)
- 1¾ tbsp (½oz/15g) all-purpose (plain) flour
- ⅛oz (4g) powdered gelatin
- 1 tbsp plus 2 tsp (24ml) cold water
- ½ cup (4¼oz/120g) mascarpone

Make the Saint-Honoré cream

Heat the milk, cream, vanilla bean, and seeds in a saucepan over a medium heat. Whisk the egg yolks with the sugar, cornstarch, and flour in a mixing bowl until very pale and thickened. Add a little of the hot milk mixture, mix with a whisk, then return all the mixture to the saucepan and bring to the boil. Remove the vanilla bean and transfer the custard to a mixing bowl. Soak the gelatin in the water, then fold it into the hot custard, mixing with a whisk. Finally, add the mascarpone and mix in.

Press plastic wrap (cling film) over the surface of the custard and, when cold, chill it for 1 hour in the refrigerator.

Make the Chantilly cream

Using an electric hand beater, whip the cream until standing in soft peaks. Whisk in the sugar, vanilla seeds, and mascarpone until the cream is holding its shape.

Roll out the pastry base

Roll out the puff pastry to a 9½-inch (24-cm) round. Chill in the refrigerator while you prepare the choux pastry.

Make the choux pastry

Bring the water, salt, sugar, and butter to the boil in a saucepan over a medium heat. Remove the pan from

Recipe continues on next page

Chantilly cream

Scant 2½ cups (19fl oz/550ml) whipping cream (35% fat)

5¾ tbsp (1¾oz/50g) powdered (icing) sugar

Seeds from 1 vanilla bean

⅔ cup (5½oz/150g) mascarpone

Pastry base

7oz (200g) puff pastry (see page 230)

Choux pastry

¾ cup plus 1 tbsp (6½fl oz/190ml) water

¼ tsp salt

¾ tsp superfine (caster) sugar

5 tbsp (2½oz/75g) butter

¾ cup plus 1½ tbsp (3¾oz/110g) all-purpose (plain) flour

6¾oz (190g) eggs

Caramel

2 cups less 2 tbsp (13oz/375g) superfine (caster) sugar

½ cup less 1 tbsp (3¾fl oz/110ml) water

3 tbsp (1¾oz/45g) liquid glucose

1 tbsp (½oz/15g) butter

the heat, add the flour in one go, then mix with a spatula until you have a smooth, soft dough. Dry it out over the heat for about 10 seconds. Transfer the dough to a bowl (this will stop the cooking). Using a spatula, gradually beat in the eggs, checking the consistency as you go. If you trace a groove in the dough, it should close up slowly.

Spoon the dough into a piping bag fitted with a ½-inch (12-mm) plain tip.

Cook the pastry base

Preheat the oven to 350°F (180°C/Gas mark 4). Place the chilled puff pastry round on a baking sheet lined with parchment paper. Pipe the choux pastry in a crown around the edges of the puff pastry. Line a second baking sheet with parchment paper and pipe about 20 choux buns on it, 1 inch (2.5cm) in diameter and spaced well apart. Pipe the rest of the choux in a spiral inside the crown to give it volume. Bake in the preheated oven for 30 minutes. When baked, cool the crown and choux buns on a wire rack.

Make the caramel

Dissolve the sugar in the water and liquid glucose in a saucepan over a medium heat. Add the butter and stir in. Remove the pan from the heat when the caramel starts to color.

To finish

Dip the bottom of the choux buns in the caramel and stick them in a ring on the Saint-Honoré crown, reserving three for decoration. Fit a piping bag with a Saint-Honoré tip, spoon in the Chantilly cream, pipe the cream inside the Saint-Honoré and place the reserved choux buns on top. Chill in the refrigerator until ready to serve.

Although he certainly did not create it, it was Antonin Carême who made the modern choux pastry recipe popular. He also set the fashion for filling choux buns with either crème pâtissière or Chantilly cream.

Choux buns
filled with Chantilly cream

•
Preparation time:
30 minutes
Cooking time:
25 to 30 minutes
•

INGREDIENTS
FOR 8 TO 10 CHOUX BUNS

14oz (400g) choux pastry dough (see page 230)
Powdered (icing) sugar, for dusting

Chantilly cream

2¼ cups (19fl oz/550ml) whipping cream (35% fat), chilled
5¾ tbsp (1¾oz/50g) powdered (icing) sugar
Dash of natural vanilla flavoring

Shape the buns

Preheat the oven to 375°F (190°C/Gas mark 5). Spoon the choux pastry dough into a piping bag fitted with a ½-inch (12-mm) plain tip. Line a baking sheet with parchment paper and pipe choux buns, 1½ inches (3.5cm) in diameter, spacing them about 1¼ inches (3cm) apart. Dust the choux buns with powdered sugar and bake for 25 to 30 minutes.

Make the Chantilly cream

Whip the chilled cream with the sugar and vanilla flavoring. Once the choux buns are baked and cooled, cut off their tops, two-thirds from their base, using a serrated knife.

Spoon the cream into a piping bag fitted with a large fluted tip. Pipe swirls of cream over the base of each bun and sit the lids on top. Dust with powdered sugar.

In the early 19th century, Antonin Carême made his own version of this cake recipe, which had originally been created across the Channel a century before. The biscuits surrounding the cake were at that time called *à la cuillère* (spoon biscuits) and the great French pastry chef also swiftly topped his charlotte with a bavarois cream when he served it at grand banquets. He named it, first of all, *à la parisienne* (Parisian style) and then *à la russe* (Russian style) to please Tsar Alexander I. Could the name "Charlotte", as this indulgent cake is called, possibly be a reference to the ruffled bonnet made popular at the time by Queen Charlotte?

Parisian chocolate charlotte

Preparation time: 1 hour
Cooking time: 18 minutes
Chilling time: 4 to 5 hours

EQUIPMENT

8½-inch (22-cm) charlotte mold

INGREDIENTS TO SERVE 6 TO 8

10½ to 12oz (300 to 350g) boudoir biscuits (see page 50)

Custard ½ cup (4fl oz/120ml) whole milk • ⅔ cup (5¼fl oz/160ml) whipping cream (35% fat) • 1 vanilla bean, slit lengthwise and seeds scraped out • 3 egg yolks • 5⅔ tbsp (2½oz/70g) superfine (caster) sugar

Chocolate bavarois cream 10½oz (300g) bittersweet (dark) chocolate (70% cacao), chopped • 6½ gelatin leaves (½oz/12.5g) • 1¾ cups (14fl oz/400ml) whipping cream

Syrup ½ cup (4fl oz/120ml) water • ⅔ cup less 1 tsp (4¼oz/120g) superfine (caster) sugar • ½ vanilla bean, slit lengthwise and seeds scraped out • 3 tbsp (¾oz/20g) unsweetened cocoa powder

For decoration and serving (optional) Chocolate shavings

Make the custard

Heat the milk and cream in a saucepan, add the vanilla bean and seeds, and bring to the boil. Take the pan off the heat, cover it and leave to infuse for 10 minutes. Whisk the egg yolks and sugar together in a mixing bowl until pale and thickened. Gradually whisk in the warm vanilla milk. Return the mixture to the saucepan and stir with a wooden spatula over a medium heat until the temperature reaches 180°F (82°C), taking care not to let it rise above that. Strain the custard into a bowl through a fine sieve or conical sieve to stop further cooking. The custard will coat the back of the spatula and, when a finger is drawn through the custard, it will leave a trace.

Make the chocolate bavarois cream

Melt the chocolate gently in a water-bath. Soak the gelatin leaves in cold water for a few minutes to soften them. Squeeze out the leaves and add them to the still-warm custard, stirring until the gelatin melts. Add the melted chocolate and mix in.

Recipe continues on next page

You can cool the mixture more quickly in a water-bath with ice cubes added. When the temperature drops to about 68°F (20°C), the chocolate cream will start to thicken. Whip the cream and gently fold it in, using a flexible spatula, to make a bavarois cream.

Make the syrup

Heat the water, sugar, ½ vanilla pod, and seeds in a saucepan and bring to the boil. Once boiling, add the cocoa powder, mixing it in with a whisk.

To assemble and decorate

Line the charlotte mold with plastic wrap (cling film) or parchment paper. Dip the boudoir biscuits in the cold syrup and line the base and the sides of the mold with them. Carefully pour in the chocolate bavarois cream. Put the mold in the refrigerator for 4 to 5 hours. Remove the charlotte from the mold and place on a serving plate.

If you wish, you can shave off curls of chocolate using a vegetable peeler to decorate the top of the charlotte.

This recipe was invented when an apprentice at the Siraudin store in the rue de la Paix accidentally poured boiling hot cream into his chocolate mixture. His appalled master called him a *ganache*, in other words an idiot! Although this fanciful legend cannot be verified, in the 1860s the Siraudin store began selling flavored sweets they called *ganaches*.

Chocolate ganache tartlets

Preparation time: 1 hour 30 minutes
Chilling time: 3 hours 45 minutes
Cooking time: 15 minutes

EQUIPMENT

4-inch (10-cm) round pastry cutter

8 deep tartlet molds

INGREDIENTS FOR 12 TARTLETS

Chocolate sweet tart pastry ⅔ cup (3¼oz/90g) all-purpose (plain) flour · ¼ cup (2¼oz/65g) butter, diced · 5 tbsp (1¾oz/45g) powdered (icing) sugar · 1½ tbsp (½oz/15g) ground almonds · 1 pinch of salt · 2½ tbsp (¾oz/20g) unsweetened cocoa powder · 1oz (25g) egg

Ganache ¾ cup (6fl oz/175ml) whipping cream (30% fat) · 3 tbsp (1¾oz/45g) acacia honey · 7oz (200g) bittersweet (dark) chocolate (65% cacao), chopped · 1½ tbsp (¾oz/22g) butter, diced

Caramel 1 tbsp plus 1 tsp (20g) acacia honey · 1 tbsp plus 2 tsp (¾oz/20g) superfine (caster) sugar · 3 tbsp (1½fl oz/40ml) whipping cream (30% fat) · 1 tbsp (½oz/15g) butter, diced

Icing and decoration 1¾oz (45g) bittersweet (dark) chocolate (70% cacao), chopped · 1 tsp sunflower oil · Chocolate decorations of your choice

Make the chocolate sweet tart pastry

Fit a stand mixer with the flat beater attachment and, on low speed, beat everything except the egg until you have a crumbly mixture. Add the egg and beat again on low speed until the ingredients come together into a smooth dough. Cover in plastic wrap (cling film) and chill for 2 hours.

Make the ganache

Heat the cream and honey in a saucepan over a medium heat and bring to the boil. Pour over the chopped chocolate, stir to mix, then let the temperature of the ganache cool to 104°F (40°C). Add the diced butter and stir in until smooth. Chill in the refrigerator until needed.

Make the caramel

Cook the honey and sugar in a saucepan over a medium heat until the sugar dissolves and the syrup is caramel colored. Heat the cream, then pour it into the caramel, mixing until combined. Leave to cool slightly, then stir in the diced butter.

Make the icing

Melt the chocolate and oil together, stirring until it is smooth.

To assemble and decorate

Roll out the tart pastry ⅒ inch (2.5mm) thick. Using the pastry cutter, stamp out eight rounds. Line the tartlet molds with the rounds. Prick the pastry bases with a fork and trim the edges neatly with a knife. Chill for 1 hour in the refrigerator.

Preheat the oven to 350°F (180°C/Gas mark 4) and bake for 15 to 20 minutes. When the tartlet cases come out of the oven turn them out of the molds. Spoon the caramel into the bottom of each one. Chill in the refrigerator for 15 minutes. Stir the ganache to ensure it is soft and smooth, then spoon it into a piping bag fitted with a ½-inch (15-mm) plain tip. Fill the tartlets with the ganache, mounding it up in the center. Chill for 30 minutes. Remove the tartlets from the refrigerator just before serving and dip the tops in the icing. Add chocolate decorations of your choice.

Religieuses

•
Preparation time:
1 hour 30 minutes
Cooking time:
30 to 45 minutes
•

INGREDIENTS FOR 12 RELIGIEUSES

Chocolate crème pâtissière 3¼ cups (26fl oz/750ml) whole milk · ¾ cup (5½oz/150g) superfine (caster) sugar · 1 vanilla bean, slit lengthwise and seeds scraped out · 4¼oz (120g) egg yolks · ⅓ cup (1¼oz/35g) cornstarch (cornflour) · 3 ⅔ tbsp (1oz/30g) all-purpose (plain) flour · 5 tbsp (2½oz/75g) butter, diced · 2½oz (70g) bittersweet (dark) chocolate (with 70% cacao), chopped

Choux pastry ¾ cup plus 1 tbsp (6½fl oz/190ml) water · ¼ tsp salt · ¾ tsp superfine (caster) sugar · 5 tbsp (2½oz/75g) butter · ¾ cup plus 1 ½ tbsp (4oz/112g) all-purpose (plain) flour · 6¾oz (190g) eggs · 1 beaten egg, to glaze

Icing and decoration 8oz (225g) fondant icing · 1¼oz (35g) bittersweet (dark) chocolate (70% cacao) · ½ cup (4½oz/125g) softened butter · ¾ cup plus 2 tbsp (4½oz/125g) powdered (icing) sugar · ½ cup (1¾oz/50g) unsweetened cocoa powder

Make the chocolate crème pâtissière

Bring the milk, half the sugar, the vanilla bean, and seeds to the boil in a saucepan. Whisk the egg yolks with the rest of the sugar in a mixing bowl until pale and thickened. Sift in the cornstarch and flour and fold in. When the milk mixture comes to the boil, remove the vanilla bean, and pour half the hot milk into the whisked egg yolk mixture. Whisk in, then pour back into the saucepan. Bring to the boil and cook for 2 to 3 minutes. Remove the pan from the heat, add the butter and chocolate and stir until incorporated. Press plastic wrap (cling film) over the surface and, when cold, chill in the refrigerator until needed.

Make the choux pastry

Bring the water, salt, sugar, and butter to the boil in a saucepan. Take the pan off the heat, add the flour in one go, then mix with a spatula until you have a soft dough. Dry out the dough over the heat for about 10 seconds. Transfer it to a mixing bowl (to stop the cooking). Gradually beat in the eggs, checking the consistency as you go. If you trace a groove in the dough, it should close up slowly.

Preheat the oven to 350°F (180°C/Gas mark 4) and line two baking sheets with parchment paper. Spoon the dough into a piping bag fitted with a ½-inch (12-mm) plain tip and pipe 12 choux buns 2 inches (5cm) in diameter onto one sheet, spacing them apart. Onto the other baking sheet, pipe 12 small buns about 1 inch (2.5cm) in diameter. Brush the buns with beaten egg to glaze, then bake for 30 to 45 minutes—you may need to remove the tray of small buns earlier as they will cook more quickly and leave the larger ones in for longer. When the buns come out of the oven, transfer them to a wire rack to cool.

Spoon the chocolate crème pâtissière into a piping bag fitted with a ½-inch (12-mm) plain tip and fill the buns with it through a hole pierced in the bottom of each one.

To finish and decorate

Make the icing by heating the fondant and chocolate in a saucepan to 95°F to 59°F (35 to 37°C). Dip the larger buns and then the smaller ones in the icing, smoothing the edges with your finger.

If wished you can also decorate with a collar. Mix the butter, sugar, and cocoa powder together and spoon into a piping bag fitted with a fluted tip. Pipe flames and a collar on the top of each large bun. Place the smaller buns on top.

In French, *une religieuse* is a nun, so what is pious about these choux buns? Maybe the crosses representing the grills on convent railings, which decorated it at the time when it was described as a tart? Today, the religieuse consists of two choux buns, one on top of the other, filled with crème pâtissière, with an irresistible collar of cream, as created by Frascati. In the 1850s, the pastry-chef and ice cream maker owned a store on the corner of the rue de Richelieu and boulevard de Montmartre and it proved a mouthwatering use of the newly invented piping bag!

A classic today in Parisian bakeries which, in 1910, would have been on the menu of *Le Bel Âge* bistro in the boulevard des Capucines. Michel Lunarca, the owner, is reputed to have suggested—purely as a way of teasing his clients—that the meat filling in the sandwich was of ... human origin! Written references to this recipe have been found that date from the end of the 19th century, but without the 'Monsieur'.

Croque-monsieur

Preparation time:
30 minutes
Cooking time:
5 to 10 minutes

INGREDIENTS
FOR 8 CROQUE-MONSIEUR

16 slices of sandwich bread
10oz (280g) cooked ham slices
¾ cup less 2 tsp (5¾oz/160g) butter

Croque-monsieur topping
2¼ cups (1lb 2½oz/520g) full-fat crème fraîche
7oz (200g) Gruyère, grated
Salt and pepper

At Delmontel, we make our own organic sandwich bread but you can buy yours at your local baker's or elsewhere. Carefully remove the crusts from the slices of bread using a serrated knife.

Make the croque-monsieur topping
Mix the crème fraîche and Gruyère together, seasoning with salt and pepper. Spread the mixture over half the bread slices. Top each with the slices of ham. Spread with another layer of the topping and cover with a second slice of bread.

Assemble
Melt the butter and brush it over the bread slices. Preheat the oven to 350°F (180°C/Gas mark 4) and bake for 5 to 10 minutes. Eat with a fresh green salad or cut each croque-monsieur into four and serve with aperitifs.

1 —— Pont-neufs
2 —— Mirlitons
3 —— Beauvilliers
4 —— Moka
Praline yule log
5 —— Millefeuille
6 —— Salambos
7 —— Apple and almond tart

Latin Quarter

When you cross the Seine to the Left Bank, you enter the Paris of cafés, a district made for strolling. Browse the bookstores on the boulevard Saint-Michel, stop for a coffee in the rue de la Huchette, and soak up the sun in the Luxembourg Gardens before climbing to the top of the Montagne Sainte-Geneviève to reach the Panthéon, where France's most illustrious citizens are laid to rest. The Latin Quarter is also the Paris of intellectuals. It is where artists and poets gather at the legendary Café de Flore to debate, communicate, and create. It is an opportunity to change the world but, most importantly, to enjoy a few pastries: a moka for coffee lovers, a millefeuille for those with a sweet tooth, or a salambo for lovers of fine literature.

The perfect example of puff pastry made the traditional way. The first recipe for millefeuille was recorded in *Le Cuisinier François* (*The French Cook*) in 1651 by François Pierre de La Varenne. In its present form, the millefeuille had its finest hour in Adolphe Seugnot's pâtisserie on the rue du Bac in the late 1860s. It was Antonin Carême who determined the number of turns, making it *la crème de la crème.*

Millefeuille

Preparation time:
45 minutes
Chilling time:
45 minutes + 45 minutes
Cooking time:
35 to 40 minutes

INGREDIENTS TO SERVE 6 TO 8

1lb 2oz (600g) puff pastry (see page 230, or buy all-butter puff pastry)

Crème pâtissière 1 cup (9fl oz/250ml) whole milk · ¼ cup (1¾oz/50g) superfine (caster) sugar · 1 vanilla bean, slit lengthwise and seeds scraped out · 1½oz (40g) egg yolks · 3½ tsp (⅓oz/10g) all-purpose (plain) flour · 2½ tbsp (½oz/15g) cornstarch (cornflour) · 2 tbsp (1oz/25g) butter

Icing 7oz (200g) white fondant icing · 1oz (30g) bittersweet (dark) chocolate

Roll out the puff pastry to a square ⅛ inch (3.5mm) thick, with sides measuring about 12 inches (30cm). Line a baking sheet with parchment paper and lift the pastry square onto it. Chill in the refrigerator for 45 minutes. Preheat the oven to 400°F (200°C/Gas mark 6) and bake the pastry for 35 to 40 minutes until it is golden brown and cooked all the way to the center. Set it aside to cool.

Make the crème pâtissière

Prepare the crème pâtissière while the pastry is baking. Heat the milk with half the sugar in a saucepan over a medium heat with the vanilla bean and seeds. Whisk the egg yolks with the rest of the sugar in a mixing bowl until pale and thickened. Sift in the flour and cornstarch. When the milk mixture is simmering, remove the vanilla bean and pour some into the whisked egg yolks and sugar. Mix, then pour the mixture back into the saucepan and stir constantly over the heat with a whisk for 1 to 2 minutes until the custard comes back to the boil. Take the saucepan off the heat and add the butter, stirring until it melts and is mixed in. Transfer the custard to a bowl, press plastic wrap (cling film) over the surface and, when cool, chill in the refrigerator for 45 minutes.

Assemble and ice

Using a serrated knife, cut the puff pastry into three rectangles each measuring 4 x 12 inches (10 × 30cm). Remove the crème pâtissière from the refrigerator and whisk lightly to soften it. Spoon the crème pâtissière into a piping bag fitted with a ½-inch (12-mm) plain tip and pipe it over one pastry rectangle. Cover with a second rectangle of pastry and repeat the piping. Place the final rectangle of pastry on top, smoothing the crème pâtissière layers evenly at the sides with a spatula.

Heat the fondant in a saucepan over a medium heat until the temperature of it reaches a maximum of 95°F to 104°F (35°C to 40°C). Using a spatula, spread the fondant over the top rectangle of pastry in an even layer. Melt the chocolate in the microwave and spoon it into a paper piping cone. Snip off the tip of the cone and pipe lines down the length of the fondant. Draw the tip of a small paring knife from one line to the next, alternating the direction each time, to create a feather pattern. Cut into 4-inch (10-cm) bars and chill in the refrigerator until ready to serve.

These small tartlets, named after the eponymous Parisian bridge, made their appearance on restaurant menus during the 19th century. A recipe for them was published in 1873 by Jules Gouffré in his *Livre Pâtisserie* and the tartlets are easily recognizable by the pastry cross sitting on top of a flavored crème pâtissière filling. A variation is also made with frangipane and named after the Pont d'Arcole. Obviously, architecture was a source of inspiration for pastry chefs!

Pont-neufs

•

Preparation time:
30 minutes
Chilling time:
1 hour
Cooking time:
15 to 20 minutes

•

EQUIPMENT

4-inch (10-cm) round pastry cutter

10 tartlet molds 3¼ inch (8cm) in diameter

INGREDIENTS TO MAKE 10 TARTLETS

12oz (350g) choux pastry dough (see page 230) · 1½ tbsp (¾oz/20ml) orange flower water · 1 egg · Redcurrant (or raspberry) jelly · Powdered (icing) sugar · Butter for the molds

Sweet shortcrust pastry 7 tbsp (3½oz/105g) butter, diced · 2 tsp (¼oz/8.5g) superfine (caster) sugar · 1 tsp (⅛oz/3.5g) salt · 1⅓ cups (6oz/175g) all-purpose (plain) flour · 2oz (55g) egg (about 1 large egg), beaten

Crème pâtissière 1 cup (8fl oz/240ml) milk · 5 tbsp (2oz/60g) sugar · 1oz (25g) egg · ¾oz (20g) egg yolk · ¼ cup (¾oz/25g) cornstarch (cornflour) · Natural vanilla flavoring, to taste

Make the sweet shortcrust pastry

Fit a stand mixer with the flat beater attachment and mix the butter, sugar, salt, and flour together on low speed until the mixture resembles breadcrumbs. Add the beaten egg and mix until you have a smooth dough. Cover the dough with plastic wrap (cling film) and chill in the refrigerator for 1 hour.

Make the crème pâtissière

Bring the milk and half the sugar to the boil in a saucepan. Whisk the egg, egg yolks, the rest of the sugar, and the vanilla flavoring in a mixing bowl. Sift in the cornstarch. When the milk is boiling, pour half onto the egg mixture, mixing with a whisk. Pour the mixture back into the saucepan and leave to boil for 2 to 3 minutes until you have a thickened, smooth custard.

Assemble and finish

Prepare the choux pastry dough following the recipe on page 230. Preheat the oven to 375°F (190°C /Gas mark 5).

Roll out the shortcrust pastry to ⅛ inch (3mm) thick and cut out 10 rounds using the pastry cutter. Reserve the pastry trimmings to make the crosses. Butter the tartlet molds and line with the pastry rounds.

Using a spatula, mix the crème pâtissière and choux pastry dough together, flavoring with the orange flower water. Spoon the mixture into a piping bag fitted with a ½-inch (12-mm) plain tip and fill the pastry cases with it. Break the egg into a ramekin, beat it, then brush it over the tartlets to glaze them. Gather together the pastry trimmings, roll out, and cut into strips ⅛ inch (3mm) thick and ⅙ inch (4 to 5mm) wide. Press two strips in a cross on top of each tartlet and bake the tartlets for 15 to 20 minutes. Leave them to cool before turning them out of the molds.

Heat a little redcurrant (or raspberry) jelly in a small saucepan over a low heat. Using a pastry brush, brush two opposite quarters with the jelly and dust the two others with powdered sugar.

Mirlitons

Guillaume Tirel, known as Taillevent, was chef to the Duke of Normandy and then to Charles V and Charles VI. In 1340 he created these special little tartlets as a tribute to the Normandy town where he was born. Taillevent is also credited with writing *Le Viandier,* the first cookbook to be published in the French language.

•

Preparation time:
30 minutes
Cooking time:
20 minutes

•

EQUIPMENT

4½ inch (11.5-cm) round fluted pastry cutter

8 *pomponnette* or tartlet molds, 3 inches (7.5cm) in diameter

INGREDIENTS
TO MAKE 8 TARTLETS

9oz (250g) puff pastry (see page 230 or buy all-butter puff pastry)

2 eggs

1 cup (3½oz/100g) ground almonds

½ cup (3½oz/100g) superfine (caster) sugar

Natural vanilla flavoring

Orange flower water

Powdered (icing) sugar

Butter for the molds

Preheat the oven to 350°F (180°C/Gas mark 4).

Roll out the puff pastry to a thickness of 1/16 inch (2mm) and cut out eight rounds using the fluted pastry cutter. Butter the tartlet molds and line with the pastry rounds.

Break the eggs into a large jug and add the ground almonds and sugar. Lightly whisk together, then add a few drops of vanilla flavoring and orange flower water, to taste. Pour this batter into the tartlet cases to fill them by three-quarters.

Dust the tartlets generously with powdered sugar and bake in the oven for about 20 minutes.

NOTE:
SEASONAL FRUITS CAN ALSO BE ADDED TO THE BATTER AND YOU CAN ADD CRUMBLED MACARONS TO EACH PASTRY CASE BEFORE POURING IN THE BATTER.

The dawn of the 19th century saw the arrival of the fashion for travelling and, therefore, *gâteaux de voyage*, cakes that can be wrapped in aluminum foil to protect them while being transported. This cake, which was among the first of such cakes, owes its name to Monier, an apprentice to the restaurateur Antoine Beauvilliers, who, upon opening his own store on rue Monsieur-le-Prince, saluted his master by creating this cake, which keeps very well.

Preparation time:
50 minutes
Cooking time:
30 minutes

EQUIPMENT

8-inch (20-cm) round cake pan

Beauvilliers

INGREDIENTS
TO SERVE 6

½ cup (1¾oz/50g) ground almonds
¾ cup plus 2 tbsp (6oz/175g) superfine (caster) sugar
Seeds of ½ vanilla bean
1½oz (40g) beaten eggs
3½ tbsp (1¾fl oz/50ml) kirsch
3 egg yolks, plus 1 whole egg
¼ cup plus ½ tbsp (1¾oz/50g) rice flour
(1½oz/45g) all-purpose (plain) flour
6 tbsp (3¼oz/90g) butter, melted and warm
4¼oz (120g) egg whites
Butter for the cake pan

Preheat the oven to 350°F (180°C/Gas mark 4). Butter the cake pan.

Using a whisk, stir the ground almonds with ¼ cup (1¾oz/50g) of the sugar in a mixing bowl. Add the vanilla seeds, then whisk in the beaten eggs and the kirsch.

In another mixing bowl, whisk the remaining sugar with the three egg yolks and whole egg. Add the almond batter and mix until combined. Sift in the rice flour and all-purpose flour, followed by the warm melted butter. Whisk everything together. In a third bowl, whisk the egg whites until standing in firm peaks.

Using a flexible spatula, gently fold the whisked whites into the batter.

Pour the batter into the prepared cake pan. Bake for 30 minutes. When the cake comes out of the oven, turn it out onto a wire rack to cool.

NOTE:
ORIGINALLY THE BEAUVILLIERS WOULD HAVE BEEN WRAPPED IN *PAPIER DE PLOMB* (LITERALLY "LEAD PAPER" BUT MADE OF TIN) FOR TRAVELING, THE FORERUNNER OF TODAY'S ALUMINUM FOIL.

HOTEL DE SEINE
FISH
BAR A VIN
B
BENSIMON

In 1863, a year after the publication of Flaubert's novel *Salammbô*, the Pâtisserie Boissier, who were expanding their number of stores into the most elegant areas of Paris, created this *petit-four*, naming it after the Carthaginian princess who was the heroine of the book. During that century, the choux buns, which were originally decorated with chopped pistachios and glazed with caramel, became a great success.

Salambos

Preparation time:
45 minutes
Resting time:
45 minutes
Cooking time:
35 minutes

INGREDIENTS TO MAKE 12 SALAMBOS

Crème pâtissière 3¼ cups (24fl oz/750ml whole milk · ¾ cup (5½oz/150g) superfine (caster) sugar · 1 vanilla bean, slit lengthwise and seeds scraped out · 4¼oz (120g) egg yolk · ⅓ cup (1¼ oz/35g) cornstarch (cornflour) · 3⅔ tbsp (1oz/30g) all-purpose (plain) flour · 5 tbsp (2½oz/75g) butter, diced

Choux pastry ¾ cup plus 1 tbsp (6½fl oz/190ml) water · ⅛ tsp (1⁄28oz/1g) salt · ¾ tsp (1⁄7oz/3g) superfine (caster) sugar · 5 tbsp (2½oz/75g) butter · ¾ cup plus 1½ tbsp (3¾oz/110g) all-purpose (plain) flour · 6¾oz (190g) eggs

For decoration 1½ cups (10½oz/300g) superfine (caster) sugar · 7 tbsp (3½fl oz/100ml) water · 12 flaked almonds

Make the crème pâtissière

Bring the milk, half the sugar, the vanilla bean, and the seeds to the boil in a saucepan over a medium heat. Whisk the egg yolks with the rest of the sugar in a mixing bowl until pale and thickened. Sift in the cornstarch and flour and fold in. When the milk mixture boils, remove the vanilla bean, and pour half the mixture over the whisked yolks. Whisk to combine, then pour back into the saucepan. Leave to boil for 2 to 3 minutes. Take the pan off the heat, add the diced butter and stir until the butter has melted and is mixed in. Press plastic wrap (cling film) over the surface, leave to cool, then chill until needed.

Make and bake the choux pastry

Preheat the oven to 400°F (200°C/Gas mark 6).

Bring the water, salt, sugar, and butter to the boil in a saucepan over a medium heat. Take the pan off the heat, add all the flour in one go, and mix in with a spatula until you have a soft dough. Dry the dough out over the heat for about 10 seconds. Scrape it into a mixing bowl (to stop the cooking). Using a spatula, gradually beat in the eggs, checking the consistency as you go. If you trace a groove in the dough, it should close up slowly.

Spoon the dough into a piping bag fitted with a ½-inch (12-mm) plain tip. Line a baking sheet with parchment paper and pipe 12 salambos on it, 1¼ inch (3cm) wide and 2¾ inches (7cm) long, spacing them apart.

Bake for 35 minutes. When the buns come out of the oven, leave them to cool on a wire rack. Remove the crème pâtissière from the refrigerator and whisk to soften it. Spoon it into a piping bag fitted with a ½-inch (12-mm) plain tip. Pierce a hole in the bottom of each salambo and pipe in the crème pâtissière to fill.

Make the caramel decoration

Heat the sugar and water in a saucepan until the sugar melts, then boil until the syrup is a light caramel. Take the pan off the heat, dip the tops of the salambos in the caramel, and top each one with a flaked almond. Transfer the salambos to a serving plate.

I was taught to make this great classic recipe when I was an apprentice at the Maison Pradier Pâtisserie in the rue de Bourgogne. It was there that I learned the ethics of my profession—a respect for products, discipline, a sense of endeavor, and hard work—which I do my best to pass on today.

Apple and almond tart

Preparation time:
30 minutes
Chilling time:
1 hour
Cooking time:
25 to 30 minutes

EQUIPMENT

8½-inch (22-cm) baking ring, 1½ inches (4cm) high

INGREDIENTS TO SERVE 8

Sweet tart pastry 1⅓ cups (6oz/175g) all-purpose (plain) flour • ¼ tsp (1g) salt • ½ cup (2¼oz/65g) powdered (icing) sugar • ¼ cup (1oz/25g) ground almonds • 7 tbsp (3½oz/105g) butter, diced • 1¼oz (35g) egg • Butter for the baking ring

Apples 3½oz (100g) Braeburn, Gala or Golden Delicious apples • ¾ cup (5½oz/150g) sugar • 7 tbsp (3½oz/100g) butter

Almond topping ½ cup plus 1¼ tbsp (4oz/115g) superfine (caster) sugar • 4oz (115g) egg whites • 4oz (115g) flaked almonds

Make the sweet tart pastry

Fit a stand mixer with the flat beater attachment. Sift the flour, salt, and powdered sugar into the bowl and add the ground almonds and diced butter. Mix on the lowest speed until the mixture is like breadcrumbs, then add the egg and mix again until you have a smooth dough. Wrap the dough in plastic wrap (cling film) and chill it in the refrigerator for 1 hour.

Prepare the apples

Peel, core, and cut the apples into small dice. Sweat them in a saucepan with the sugar and butter over a medium heat. Cook for 10 to 15 minutes. The apples must be cooked but still hold their shape and not be reduced to a compote. Set aside to cool then store in the refrigerator until needed.

Make the almond topping

Put the sugar, egg whites, and almonds in a bowl and mix together using a spatula.

To assemble

Preheat the oven to 350°F (180°C/Gas mark 4).

Roll out the pastry ⅛ inch (3mm) thick and cut into a round 12 inches (30cm) in diameter.

Generously butter the pastry ring, place it on a baking sheet, and line the pastry into it, trimming the top edge neatly. Spoon the apples into the pastry case and pour the almond topping over them, spreading it in an even layer with the back of a spoon.

Bake for 25 to 30 minutes. When the tart comes out of the oven, leave it to cool, before transferring it to serving plate and lifting off the ring.

Preparation time:
1 hour
Chilling time:
30 minutes
Cooking time:
30 minutes

EQUIPMENT

8-inch (20-cm) round cake pan

Moka

INGREDIENTS
TO SERVE 8

Genoese sponge

5½oz (150g) eggs
5⅔ tbsp (2½oz/70g) superfine (caster) sugar
¾ tbsp (⅓oz/10g) honey
1½ tbsp (¾oz/20g) butter, plus 1½ tbsp (¾oz/20g) for the cake pan
⅔ cup less 1 tbsp (2¾oz/80g) all-purpose (plain) flour
Natural vanilla flavoring

Buttercream

½ cup plus 2 tbsp (4¼oz/120g) superfine (caster) sugar
3½ tbsp (1¾oz/50ml) water
3½oz (100g) eggs
⅔ cup (3½oz/150g) butter, diced and softened
1 cup (1fl oz/30ml) espresso coffee
1 tsp instant coffee (optional)

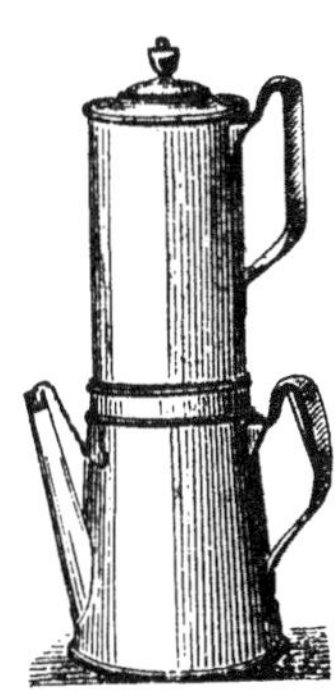

Make the Genoese sponge

Preheat the oven to 350°F (180°C/Gas mark 4).

Sit a stainless steel bowl in a water-bath. Add the eggs, sugar, and honey and, using an electric hand beater, whisk until the mixture is warm and mousse-like. Remove the bowl from the water-bath and continue to whisk for 7 to 8 minutes until the bowl and mixture are completely cold. Reduce the speed to very low and whisk for a further 10 minutes. The batter must be very light and fall in a ribbon from a spatula.

Melt the butter, reserving 1½ tablespoons to grease the cake pan. Sift the flour and gently fold it into the batter using a flexible spatula. Next fold in the vanilla flavoring, to taste, and then the melted butter until smooth. Grease the cake pan with the reserved butter. Pour the batter into the pan, place the pan in the oven immediately, and bake for 30 minutes. Turn out the cake and leave it to cool on a wire rack.

Make the buttercream

Put the sugar and water in a saucepan over a high heat. When the sugar has dissolved, boil the syrup until the temperature reaches 250°F (120°C). Fit a stand mixer with the whisk attachment and whisk the egg whites until standing in firm peaks. Pour the sugar syrup into the egg whites and whisk on full speed for 2 to 3 minutes. Lower the speed and add the diced butter, continuing to whisk for a few more minutes. Pour in the coffee. You can add a spoonful of instant coffee to boost the flavor.

Recipe continues on next page

Make the coffee syrup

Heat the water and sugar in a saucepan until the sugar dissolves, then bring to the boil. Add the espresso and freeze-dried coffee. Mix, then leave to cool.

Assemble and decorate

Cut the sponge horizontally into three equal layers. Soften the buttercream, if necessary. Place one slice of cake on a board and brush it with the syrup. Spread with an even layer of buttercream. Brush a second layer of sponge with syrup, place it on top of the first, and spread with buttercream. Finish with the third sponge layer, brush it with syrup, and spread the top and sides of the cake with the remaining buttercream. You can decorate the top of the cake by tracing random lines in the buttercream with a serrated knife.

Coat the sides of the cake with the chopped toasted almonds. Chill the cake in the refrigerator for at least 30 minutes before serving.

Coffee syrup

7 tbsp (3½fl oz/100ml) water
½ cup (3½oz/100g) superfine (caster) sugar
½ cup (½fl oz/15ml) espresso coffee
½ tsp instant coffee

For decoration

Chopped toasted almonds

Was it Quillet or Rémondet who invented chocolate-flavored moka coffee? The airy cream that flavors the sponge cake is attributed to Quillet, a 19th century pastry chef based on rue de Buci, but was it the work of his successor Rémondet? Another theory is that Guignard, who may have worked in this pâtisserie, may also have invented it. One thing is certain: the moka had the good taste to be born in the mid-19th century!

LES EDITEURS
café
restaurant

Praline yule log
(Bûche de Noël)

Preparation time:
2 hours
Chilling time:
1 hour
Cooking time:
5 to 6 minutes

INGREDIENTS TO SERVE 8 TO 10

Rolled sponge 1 tbsp plus 2 tsp (1oz/25g) butter • 4 egg yolks • 6 tbsp (2½oz/75g) superfine (caster) sugar • ½ cup plus 1 tbsp (2½oz/75g) all-purpose (plain) flour • 3 egg whites

Syrup ¼ cup (2fl oz/60ml) water • 3¼ tbsp (1½oz/40g) superfine (caster) sugar • ½ vanilla bean, slit lengthwise and seeds scraped out

Praline buttercream 1 cup plus 3 tbsp (8½oz/235g) superfine (caster) sugar • 4½oz (125g) eggs • 1¾ cups less 1 tbsp (13¾oz/390g) butter, diced and softened • 5½oz (150g) praline

Make the rolled sponge

Preheat the oven to 350°F (175°C/Gas mark 4).

Melt the butter in a saucepan over a low heat.

Fit a stand mixer with the whisk attachment and whisk the egg yolks with the sugar on medium speed for 5 minutes. Sift in the flour, add the melted butter, and fold in.

Whisk the egg whites until standing in firm peaks and gently fold them into the yolk mixture with a flexible spatula.

Line a baking sheet with parchment paper and spread the batter over it. Take care not to deflate the batter by spreading it too flat; it needs to be about ⅝ inch (1.5cm) thick. Bake for 5 to 6 minutes. When the sponge comes out of the oven, turn it over onto a clean dish towel and peel off the parchment paper.

Make the syrup

Heat the water with the sugar, vanilla bean, and seeds in a saucepan over a medium heat until the sugar dissolves.

Make the praline buttercream

Put the sugar in a saucepan, cover it with water, and melt the sugar over a medium heat. Cook until the temperature of the syrup reaches 250°F (120°C).

In a mixing bowl, whisk the eggs using an electric hand beater until they are very pale. Pour in the syrup in a thin, steady stream, continuing to whisk until the mixture is completely cold. Add the diced butter and then the praline, mixing until combined.

Assemble

Using a brush, coat the cold sponge with the syrup. Spread the praline buttercream over the sponge with a palette knife, reserving one quarter of the buttercream for decoration. Tightly roll up the sponge and chill in the refrigerator for about 1 hour.

Once the roll is well chilled, cut a slice off one end, about ¾ inch (2cm) thick. Place it on the log at an angle to look like a sawn-off branch.

Using a palette knife, spread the log with the remaining praline buttercream to cover it completely. Draw the knife down the length of the log to imitate the bark of a tree. You can accentuate the bark by running a fork dipped in hot water over the buttercream.

In the 1870s, logs moved from the fireside to the table! Various pastry chefs laid claim to inventing the yule log, whether in Poitou, where it was originally made with chestnuts, or in Paris, where it was a sponge cake flavored with coffee or chocolate. Among its potential creators, we can point to Charabot, a pastry chef on the rue de Buci, and an apprentice working in Saint-Germain-des Prés. Also, Pierre Lacam, head of Maison Ladurée, at the time the pastry chef of the Prince of Monaco, who went into partnership with his son-in-law to open Maison Seurre on the rue des Martyrs, and in 1900 published the first recipe for a yule log.

PLACE
SAINT-GERMAIN
DES PRÉS
LES DEUX MAGOTS
LES DEUX MAGOTS
CAFÉ LITTÉRA

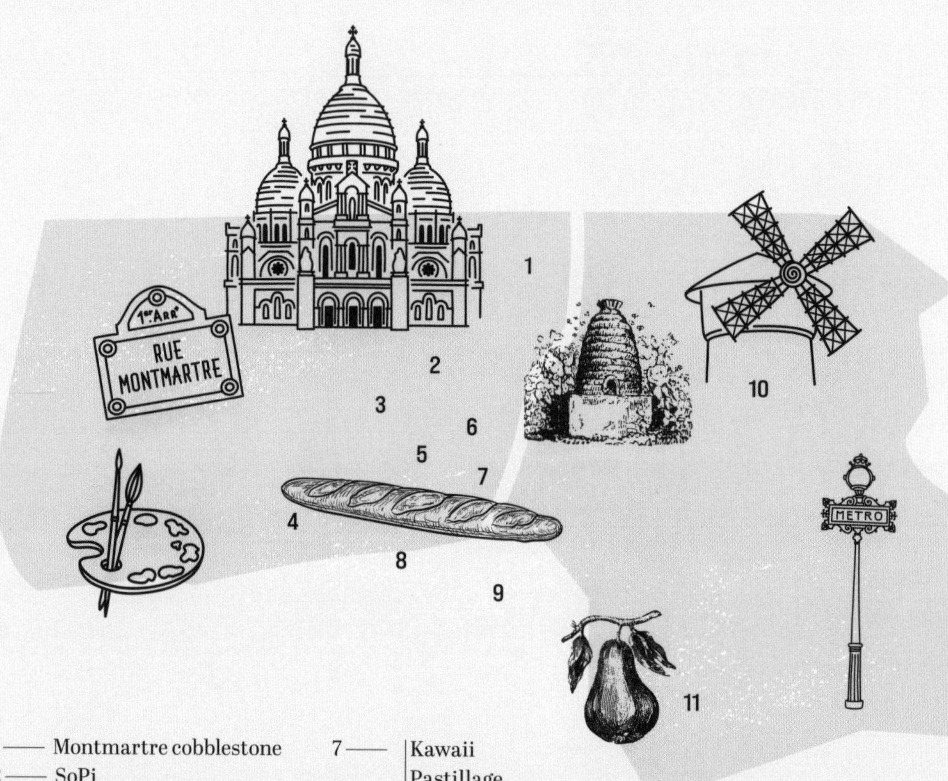

1 —— Montmartre cobblestone
2 —— SoPi
3 —— Saint-George
4 —— Josephine
5 —— Marquise
6 —— Baguettes
Flaky rye bread
with honey
7 —— Kawaii
Pastillage
8 —— Tarte Bourdaloue
9 —— 100%
Gauguin
10 —— Condorcet
11 —— Pear Belle-Hélène

From Pigalle to Montmartre

As you make your way down Montmartre's steep, cobbled lanes, you can feel the air of freedom and creativity blowing through its narrow streets, lit by the neon theatre and cabaret signs. The Sacré-Coeur towers above it all, illuminating this artistic quartier. A powerful bastion of inspiration for Arnaud Delmontel, it is an area in which pâtisserie endlessly reinvents itself. Rich in the creations of the past, it still pursues its quest for modernity. Paris never stops inspiring Parisians!

Baguettes

Preparation time: 30 minutes • Resting time: about 3 hours
Cooking time: 25 minutes

INGREDIENTS TO MAKE 10 BAGUETTES

7¾ cups (60fl oz/1.75 litres) water
(70% of the quantity of flour)
3¼ tbsp (1½oz/40g) salt
1oz (26g) baker's (fresh) yeast
19¼ cups (5lb 8oz/2.5kg) T55 flour

TO MAKE GOOD BREAD DOUGH, THE SUM OF THE TEMPERATURES OF THE FLOUR, THE BAKERY, AND THE WATER MUST BE 60°C (140°F). FOR EXAMPLE, IF THE BAKERY IS 25°C (77°F) AND THE FLOUR 20°C (68°F), THE TEMPERATURE OF THE WATER MUST BE 15°C (59°F).

Fit a stand mixer with the dough hook attachment and put the water, salt, yeast, and then the flour in the bowl. Knead for 8 minutes on the lowest speed. The temperature of the dough must be no higher than 72°F (22°C).

Leave the dough to rise in the mixer bowl for about 1 hour. After an hour, switch on the mixer for 10 seconds to fold the dough over. Repeat this three times, each 20 minutes apart. After the third time, transfer the dough to another bowl and chill in the refrigerator at 39°F (4°C).

Take the chilled dough out of the refrigerator and leave it to come up to a room temperature of 66°F (19°C).

Using a dough docker, divide the dough into pieces, each weighing 14oz (400g). Leave to rest for 20 minutes. Shape the pieces into baguettes, separating them with clean dish towels, and leave to prove for 30 to 40 minutes.

Score the tops of the baguettes with a razor blade.

Preheat the oven to 475°F (250°C/Gas mark 9) and bake the baguettes for 25 minutes. To improve their appearance, pour half a glass of water into a roasting pan placed at the bottom of the oven (be careful not to burn yourself) to produce steam—this will ensure the baguettes are golden brown when baked.

À la Renaissance is the name that appears on the neoclassical sign outside our landmark store in the rue des Martyrs. It was the obvious choice when it came to naming our traditional baguette, which in 2007 won us the accolade of best baguette in Paris. During that year, our bread graced the tables of the Élysée Palace and today Parisians and tourists can still bite into the crust of our bread that is seasoned with *sel de Guérande*. The tradition of a loaf of bread being long rather than round goes back to the 18th century when Parisians became increasingly fond of "heavy" breads. It wasn't until 1904 that the word *baguette* appeared for the first time in a manual, but its length had not yet been decided and the *grignes* (the score marks on the rounded top) were not consistent. Our baguette, the rules for which have now been codified, did not have to wait to be added to UNESCO's Intangible Cultural Heritage of Humanity List in 2022 to become emblematic of French style!

nat & nin

This rye bread, made in the same way as croissants, having several layers of butter and honey, is a cross between French breadmaking and Viennoiserie. It is one of our specialities.

Flaky rye bread

with honey

Preparation time: 30 minutes • Resting time: 4 hours 15 minutes
Cooking time: 20 to 25 minutes

INGREDIENTS TO MAKE 3 × 12OZ (350G) LOAVES

1¾ cups (8½oz/230g) rye flour
1¾ cups plus 2 tbsp (9oz/250g) T55 flour
2½ tsp (⅓oz/10g) salt
⅓oz (10g) baker's (fresh) yeast
6 tbsp (3½oz/100g) acacia honey
1 cup plus 3 tbsp (9½fl oz/275ml) water

For laminating

¾ cup plus 2 tsp (6¼oz/180g) butter, in one block
(preferably AOC Charentes-Poitou butter)

Weigh out all the dough ingredients and put them in the bowl of a stand mixer fitted with the dough hook attachment. Knead on low speed for 2 minutes, then increase the speed to medium and knead for a further 10 minutes. Cover the dough in plastic wrap (cling film) and leave it to rest in the refrigerator for 2 hours.

Roll the dough into a 12-inch (30-cm) square. Pound the laminating butter into a slightly smaller square using a rolling pin and place it on the dough. Wrap the dough around the butter like an envelope (see puff pastry technique, page 230) and give it three turns by rolling the dough to a rectangle, folding it in three and then repeating this three times. Wrap the dough in plastic wrap and chill in the refrigerator for 30 minutes between each turn. After the third turn, roll out the dough again and form it into a sausage shape. Cut it into three loaves, each weighing 12oz (350g), shaping them into ovals. Score the tops at regular intervals with a razor blade. Leave to rise for 45 minutes at 77 to 86°F (25 to 30°C).

Preheat the oven to 400°F (200°C/Gas mark 6). Place the loaves on a baking sheet and bake them for 20 to 25 minutes.

18e Arr.
RUE SAINT RUSTIQUE
Depuis 1925
LA BONNE FRANQUETTE
Anciennement
"AUX BILLARDS EN BOIS"
Cette auberge est célèbre depuis 1890
Rendez-vous d'artistes, elle a accueilli
DIAZ
PISSARO, SISLEY, DEGAS
CEZANNE, TOULOUSE-LAUTREC
RENOIR, MONET, ZOLA...
SON JARDIN SERVIT DE MODÈLE À
'VAN GOGH'
pour son tableau célèbre
'LA GUINGUETTE'
Peint en octobre 1886 et exposé maintenant au
MUSÉE D'ORSAY
Aimer, Manger, Boire et Chanter!!!
CAFÉ RESTAU
18
SIÈGE SOCIAL
République Montmartre
COUPE DU MEILLEUR POT

LA CAVE DE
LA BONNE FRANQUETTE
INTERDIT
SAUF CYCLISTE
VINS
Aimer,
Boire et Chanter !!!
LA BONNE
FRANQUETTE

Tarte Bourdaloue

•
Preparation time: 1 hour
Chilling time:
1 to 2 hours
Cooking time:
35 minutes
•

EQUIPMENT

8½-inch (22-cm) tart ring

INGREDIENTS TO SERVE 8

Pears in syrup
• 4¼ cups (35fl oz/1 litre) water • 3¾ cups (1lb 10oz/750g) superfine (caster) sugar • ½ vanilla bean, slit lengthwise and seeds scraped out • 5 or 6 pears (Passe-Crassane, Comice or Conference)

Sweet tart pastry 1 cup less 1 tbsp (4½oz/125g) all-purpose (plain) flour • 6¾ tbsp (2¼oz/65g) powdered (icing) sugar • ¼ cup (2oz/60g) butter, diced, plus extra for the tart ring • ¼ tsp salt • 1oz (30g) egg, beaten

Frangipane ¼ cup (2oz/60g) softened butter • 5 tbsp (2oz/60g) superfine (caster) sugar • 2oz (60g) eggs • ½ cup (2oz/60g) ground almonds • 3½ tsp (⅓oz/10g) all-purpose (plain) flour • ½ vanilla bean, slit lengthwise and seeds scraped out • 1 tsp sugarcane juice rum

For decoration ¾ to 1oz (20 to 30g) flaked almonds • Powdered (icing) sugar

Make the pears in syrup

It is better to prepare the pear halves in syrup yourself rather than buy canned ones.

Heat the water, sugar, vanilla bean, and seeds in a saucepan until the sugar melts. Wash and peel the pears and discard the stalks. Cut the pears in half lengthwise and remove the cores. Lower the pear halves into the syrup and poach for about 15 minutes. Check to see if the pears are tender with the point of a sharp knife. Set aside to cool in the syrup.

Make the sweet tart pastry

Sift the flour and sugar together, add the diced butter, and work the ingredients together with your fingertips until the mixture has a crumbly texture. Add the salt and egg and mix to make a smooth dough. Shape the dough into a ball, cover it in plastic wrap (cling film), and chill in the refrigerator for 1 to 2 hours.

Roll out the dough ⅛ inch (3mm) thick. Butter the tart ring, place it on a baking sheet, and line it with the pastry, trimming the top level. Prick the base lightly with a fork and chill until needed.

Make the frangipane

In the bowl of a stand mixer fitted with the whisk attachment, or in a mixing bowl and using an electric hand beater, whisk the softened butter and sugar together until light and creamy. Beat in the eggs and ground almonds, followed by the flour. Soak the vanilla seeds in the rum, then pour the vanilla-flavored rum into the almond batter. Mix and chill until needed.

To assemble and bake

Preheat the oven to 350°F (180°C/Gas mark 4).

Spread the almond batter into the tart shell, using a spatula. Drain the pears and cut the halves crosswise into thin slices, keeping the shape of the pears. Slide a small palette knife under each sliced pear half and lift it on top of the almond cream, arranging like the petals of a flower. Press the tops of the slices lightly to fan them out. Sprinkle the flaked almonds in the center and around the edges between the pears. Bake in the oven for 35 minutes.

When the tart is baked, remove it from the oven, and leave to cool before removing the ring. Dust with powdered sugar, if you'd like.

Around 1860, Nicolas Bourgoin, pastry chef at the Maison Lesserteur pâtisserie on rue Bourdaloue in the 9th arrondissement of present-day Paris, created a cake that drew attention for being almond based but without having any fruit. At the time, almond-flavored desserts were very fashionable with Parisian pastry chefs. When he took over Maison Lesserteur, it is said Fasquelle named his creation *bourdaloue*, adding a pastry case and filling it with apricots, later to be replaced by pears. In the beginning, a cross of toasted macarons decorated the early tarts, which paid homage to Father Bourdaloue, a Jesuit preacher in the 17th century, who did nothing in the tart's history but lend his name to it!

odak
GRENOUILLES

SoPi

In 2010, I teamed up with designer Amélie G to create a "spicy" cake for Valentine's Day. Wrapped in lace and great fun, SoPi is a reference to the district of "South Pigalle" where our flagship store is located.

•

Preparation time:
1 hour 30 minutes
Freezing time:
2 hours
Cooking time:
5 to 10 minutes

•

EQUIPMENT

2½-inch (6.5-cm) plain round pastry cutter

2½-inch (6.5-cm) baking ring, 4½ inches (12cm) high

Acetate sheet for baking

INGREDIENTS TO SERVE 2 (MAKES 1 CAKE)

Flour-free chocolate sponge 2½oz (70g) egg whites • 5 ⅔ tbsp (2½oz/70g) superfine (caster) sugar • 1¾oz (50g) egg yolks • ¼ cup (¾oz/20g) ground almonds • ¼ cup (¾oz/20g) raw cacao powder, sifted

Syrup ¼ cup (1¾oz/50g) superfine (caster) sugar • 3½ tbsp (1¾fl oz/50ml) water • 2 tsp (⅛oz/5g) Espelette chili powder

Chocolate and Espelette chili mousse 6oz (170g) bittersweet (dark) chocolate (70% cacao), chopped • ⅓ cup (2¾fl oz/80ml) whole milk • 2 tsp (⅛oz/5g) Espelette chili powder • ¾oz (20g) egg yolks • 4¼oz (120g) egg whites • 1 tbsp plus 2 tsp (¾oz/20g) superfine (caster) sugar

For decoration 9oz (250g) white chocolate • Red liposoluble food coloring, as needed

Make the flour-free chocolate sponge

Preheat the oven to 375°F (190°C/Gas mark 5). Whisk the egg whites with the sugar until standing in firm peaks. Add the egg yolks, ground almonds and cacao powder and gently mix them in. Line a baking sheet with parchment paper, and, using a spatula, spread the batter over it in a 6¼-inch (16-cm) square. Bake for 5 to 10 minutes. The sponge must still be soft when cooked.

Make the syrup

Heat the sugar and water in a saucepan over a medium heat. When the sugar has dissolved, bring to the boil, then add the chili powder. Cool and then store in the refrigerator.

Chocolate and Espelette chili mousse

Melt the chopped chocolate in a heatproof bowl set over a pan of gently simmering water. Heat the milk in a saucepan over a medium heat and add the chili powder. Remove the pan from the heat, cover it, and leave the milk to infuse for 15 minutes. Pour the warm milk over the chocolate, mix, and then cool until the temperature drops to 68 to 77°F (20 to 25°C). Whisk in the egg yolks. Using an electric hand beater, whisk the egg whites with the sugar to firm peaks. Delicately fold the whisked whites into the chocolate mixture.

To assemble

Using the pastry cutter, cut out three rounds from the sponge. Brush them with the chili syrup. Place one round of sponge in the baking ring. Using a piping bag or a spoon, cover the sponge with half the chocolate mousse. Lay a second sponge round on top and cover with the rest of the mousse, spreading it evenly. Put the third sponge round on top, then freeze for 2 hours until solid.

Melt the white chocolate until the temperature of it reaches 95°F (35°C), then add the red food coloring and mix with a spatula until the chocolate is evenly tinted. Cut a sheet of acetate for baking that will fit around the diameter of the cake and extend just above it in height. Fill a paper piping cone with the red-colored chocolate, snip off the tip, and pipe a lacy pattern over the plastic sheet (to look like the patterns of fishnet stockings). Allow it to set a little bit so it doesn't run when you pick up the sheet, but it should still be soft enough to bend the sheet without it breaking.

Take the cake out of the freezer, remove the baking ring, and wrap the piped chocolate band around it. When the chocolate comes into contact with the frozen cake, it will harden immediately and you will be able to pull away the plastic sheet. Serve immediately.

Our Marquise cake was created in 2008 in our store in the rue Saint-Georges. As seen in the photograph, the lady on the cake is deliciously dressed in a chocolate shell, which replicates one of the fabrics by Judith Lacrois, a local clothing designer, with a meringue crinoline under her chocolate and hazelnut ganache petticoat, decorated with candied lemon zest. A simpler version of this cake can be found below.

Marquise

Preparation time:
1 hour 30 minutes
Chilling time:
24 hours
Freezing time:
45 minutes
Cooking time:
1 hour 30 minutes

EQUIPMENT

Silpat® silicone cone, 4½ inches (12cm) in diameter and 6 inches (15cm) high
Acetate sheet for baking
Figurine (optional)

INGREDIENTS TO SERVE 8

Dark chocolate and lemon Chantilly cream 2 cups (16fl oz/450ml) whipping cream (35% fat) · 1oz (25g) lemon zest · 5½oz (160g) bittersweet (dark) chocolate (60% cacoa), chopped

French meringue 4½oz (125g) egg whites · ⅔ cup less 2 tsp (4½oz/125)g superfine (caster) sugar · ¾ cup plus 2 tbsp (4½oz/125g) powdered (icing) sugar

To assemble 10½oz (300g) bittersweet (dark) chocolate

Make the dark chocolate and lemon Chantilly cream

The day before, bring the cream to the boil in a saucepan over a high heat. Add the lemon zest and stir to mix. Once the cream is simmering, remove the pan from the heat and pour it over the chopped chocolate. Mix with a hand whisk or handheld blender until smooth. Cool and then chill the cream in the refrigerator at 39°F (4°C) for 24 hours.

Make the French meringue

Preheat the oven to 200°F (90°C/Gas mark ¼).

Whisk the egg whites to soft peaks, adding the superfine sugar in two batches whilst whisking. When the whites are standing in firm peaks, sift in the powdered sugar in two batches, whisking constantly. Spoon the meringue into a piping bag fitted with a ½-inch (15-mm) tip. Line a baking sheet with parchment paper and pipe three rounds of meringue, 2½, 3¼, and 4½ inches (6, 8, and 12cm) in diameter onto it, followed by pretty swirls in the shape of a rose for the top of the dress.

Bake for 1 hour 30 minutes.

Assemble

Fit a stand mixer with the whisk attachment and whip the dark chocolate and lemon Chantilly cream. Spread about half over the underside of the 2-½ inch (6-cm) meringue round. Place the 3¼-inch (8-cm) meringue round on top and cover that with the remaining cream. Top with the 4½-inch (12-cm) meringue. Freeze for 45 minutes.

To make the chocolate dress, melt the dark chocolate to a temperature of 104 to 113°F (40 to 45°C). Using a spatula, spread a thin layer of melted chocolate over the sheet of acetate the same height as the inside of the cone, and place it over the unmolded frozen meringue layers. Top with the meringue rosette, followed by the figurine, if you have one.

In 1864, Offenbach's *La Belle Hélène* opened in Paris and inspired several of the capital's pastry chefs to borrow the name of the operetta and create dishes they hoped would be as big a success. Caught up in the craze, Auguste Escoffier is said to have created this recipe for *Poire Belle-Helène*.

Pear Belle-Hélène

Preparation time: 35 minutes
Infusing time: 30 minutes
Cooking time: 20 minutes

INGREDIENTS TO SERVE 6

Vanilla ice cream 1¼ cups (10½fl oz/300ml) whole milk · 1½ cups (12fl oz/350ml) whipping cream (35% fat) · 1 vanilla bean, slit lengthwise and seeds scraped out · 7 egg yolks · ¾ cup (5½oz/150g) superfine (caster) sugar

Pears 6 Passe-Cressane, Conference or Comice pears · 3¼ cups (26fl oz/750ml) water · 2½ cups (1lb 2oz/500g) superfine (caster) sugar · Juice of ½ lemon · 1 vanilla bean

Chocolate sauce ¼ cup (2fl oz/60ml) water · 4½oz (125g) bittersweet (dark) chocolate (65% cacao), chopped into small pieces · ¼ cup (2fl oz/60ml) whipping cream with (35% fat)

Make the vanilla ice cream

Bring the milk and cream to the boil in a saucepan over a medium heat. Add the vanilla bean and seeds, remove the pan from the heat, and leave to infuse for 30 minutes, then strain.

Whisk the egg yolks and the sugar together on high speed. Pour over some of the vanilla milk, mix, then return to the saucepan. Stir over the heat, as for making a custard, until the temperature of the cream mixture reaches 181°F (83°C). Allow to cool. Transfer the custard to an ice-cream maker and churn according to the manufacturer's instructions. Once the ice cream is made, prepare the pears.

Cook the pears

Peel the pears, leaving them whole and without removing the stems. Bring the water, sugar, and lemon juice to the boil in a saucepan large enough to take all the pears, and add the vanilla bean (you can reuse the one from making the custard for the ice cream). Once the sugar has dissolved, lower the pears into the syrup and poach them over a medium heat for 20 minutes. Drain the pears, and leave to cool, then refrigerate.

Make the chocolate sauce

Bring the water to the boil in a saucepan, then add the chopped chocolate. Leave the chocolate to melt over a medium heat, then add the cream and mix it in with a whisk.

Serve

Place a scoop of vanilla ice cream on each dessert plate. Sit a pear alongside and coat with the warm chocolate sauce. Serve immediately.

I've chosen these two ingredients—chocolate and banana—as a tribute to Josephine Baker. She first sang her 1930 song *"J'ai deux amours: mon pays et Paris"* ("I have two loves: my country and Paris") at the Casino de Paris in the 9th arrondissement.

Josephine

•

Preparation time:
2 hours
Cooking time:
30 minutes

•

EQUIPMENT

8½-inch (22-cm) square baking frame or 12-inch (30-cm) baking ring

INGREDIENTS TO SERVE 8

Hazelnut streusel ½ cup (2oz/55g) ground hazelnuts · ¼ cup (1¾oz/50g) superfine (caster) sugar · 3½ tbsp (1¾oz/48g) butter, melted · 6 tbsp (1¾oz/48g) all-purpose (plain) flour

Banana cream 1½oz (40g) peeled banana · 3½oz (100g) mashed banana · 1½ tbsp (¾oz/20g) passion fruit pulp · 2¼oz (64g) eggs · 1⅔oz (46g) egg yolks · 1½ tbsp (1oz/24g) honey · ⅛oz (6g) gelatin leaves · ¼ cup (2oz/60g) butter, diced

Chocolate mousse ½oz (15g) egg yolk · 1¼ tsp (⅛oz/5g) superfine (caster) sugar · 2½ tbsp (1½fl oz/40ml) whole milk · ½ cup plus 1 tbsp (4½fl oz/135ml) whipping cream (35% fat) · 1oz (30g) bittersweet (dark) chocolate (70% cacao), chopped · 3½oz (100g) milk couverture chocolate, chopped

To finish Cocoa powder, for dusting (optional) · Chocolate icing (optional)

Make the hazelnut streusel

Preheat the oven to 300°F (150°C/Gas mark 2).

Using a spatula, mix together the ground hazelnuts and sugar in a bowl. Add the melted butter and flour, stirring to make a paste. Line a baking sheet with parchment paper and spread the streusel paste over it, ½ inch (1cm) thick. Bake for 15 to 20 minutes.

Make the banana cream

Chop the banana into small dice and mix them with the mashed banana and passion fruit pulp.

Whisk the eggs and egg yolks in a bowl with the honey. Transfer to a saucepan, add the mashed banana mixture and stir over the heat, as for making a crème pâtissière, until boiling.

Soak the gelatin leaves in cold water. Once softened, squeeze the excess water out of the leaves and stir into the still-hot banana cream. Add the butter and stir in until melted. Line the baking frame or ring with plastic wrap (cling film) and pour the cream into it, no more than ½ inch (1cm) thick. Chill in the refrigerator.

Make the chocolate mousse

Whisk the egg yolk with the sugar. Heat the milk and 2 tbsp (1fl oz/30ml) cream in a saucepan. Pour a little of the hot milk and cream over the egg yolk and sugar, whisk to combine, then pour the mixture back into the saucepan. Heat until the temperature reaches 180°F (82°C), stirring as for making a custard. Pour the custard over the chopped chocolates and mix well with a whisk until smooth. Whip the remaining cream, then whisk it into the chocolate custard.

Assemble

Remove the banana cream from the baking frame or ring, discarding the plastic wrap. Crumble the streusel mixture into the frame or ring in an even layer. Spoon half the chocolate mousse on top, smoothing it level. Place the banana cream on top and cover with the rest of the chocolate mousse. Smooth the surface, then chill thoroughly in the refrigerator.

To finish, you can simply dust the surface with cocoa powder or cover it with chocolate icing.

Take a stroll in the 9th arrondissement and you will discover the 4th century martyr Saint George, both in the street and the square named after him.

Saint-George

Preparation time: 2 hours
Cooking time: 10 to 12 minutes
Freezing time: 2 to 3 hours

EQUIPMENT

8½-inch (22-cm) baking ring

INGREDIENTS TO SERVE 8

Boudoir biscuits 3½oz (100g) egg whites · 7 tbsp (3oz/85g) superfine (caster) sugar · 2¼oz (65g) egg yolks · ⅔ cup (3oz/85g) all-purpose (plain) flour

Syrup 2 tbsp plus 2 tsp (1½fl oz/40ml) water · 3¼ tbsp (1½oz/40g) superfine (caster) sugar · ½ vanilla bean, slit lengthwise and seeds scraped out

Vanilla bavarois ½ cup (4½fl oz/125ml) whole milk · 1¼ cups (10½fl oz/300ml) whipping cream (35% fat) · ½ vanilla bean, slit lengthwise and seeds scraped out · 1¾oz (50g) egg yolks · ¼ cup (1¾oz/50g) superfine (caster) sugar · ⅛oz (5g) powdered gelatin · 2½ tbsp (36ml) cold water

For decoration 9oz (250g) red and black berries and currants plus 2oz (60g) for the filling · ½ pear, cored, and sliced · 5¾ tbsp (1¾oz/50g) powdered sugar

Make the boudoir biscuits

Preheat the oven to 350°F (180°C/Gas mark 4).

Fit a stand mixer with the whisk attachment and whisk the egg whites to firm peaks, adding the sugar in two batches as you whisk. Add the egg yolks, then sift in the flour and fold in using a flexible spatula. Line a baking sheet with parchment paper. Spoon the batter into a piping bag fitted with a ½-inch (12-mm) plain tip and pipe short lines of batter—side by side and touching—so that you end up with a 2 x 28-inch (70-cm) sheet of piped batter (or two 2 x 14-cm/ 5 x 35-cm sheets, depending on the size of your oven) imitating the shape of boudoir biscuits. Also pipe a round of batter, 8 inches (20cm) in diameter for the base of the dessert. Bake for 10 to 12 minutes, then transfer to a wire rack to cool.

Make the syrup

Heat the water and sugar in a saucepan with the vanilla bean and seeds and, when the sugar has dissolved, bring to the boil. Set aside.

Make the vanilla bavarois

Bring the milk, ½ cup (4½fl oz/125ml) of the cream, the vanilla bean and seeds to the boil over a medium heat. Whisk the egg yolks and sugar together in a mixing bowl until pale and thick. Whisk the hot milk mixture into the yolks and sugar in a thin, steady, stream, then pour it back into the saucepan and cook until the temperature reaches 180°F (82°C), stirring with a wooden spatula. Soak the gelatin in the water to rehydrate it, then stir it into the custard. Leave to cool to 68°F (20°C) at room temperature. Whip the remaining cream until it is standing in firm peaks.

Assemble

Put the baking ring on a serving plate or cake board. Place the biscuit round in the ring and brush it with the syrup. Arrange the line of boudoir biscuits in a circle around the edge with the rounded tops against the sides of the ring.

Whisk the custard with the whipped cream to make a bavarois. Spoon half the bavarois into the ring and top with the 2oz (60g) of the red and black fruits. Top with the remaining bavarois and freeze for 2 to 3 hours. Remove the dessert from the freezer and decorate the top with the remaining red and black fruits and pear slices.

Remove the baking ring, dust with powdered sugar, if wished, and serve.

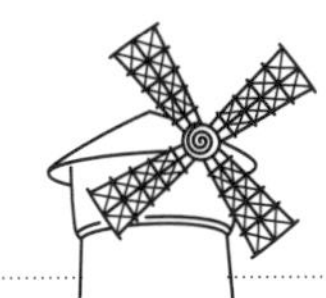

What would Montmartre be without its cobblestones, polished by the feet of so many pedestrians? First made of stone or wood, then sandstone or granite, cobblestones charted the history of the capital's urbanization before becoming improvised weapons during the riots of May 1968. This lemon and poppy seed cake, created in our Abbesses store, pays tribute to this symbol of old Paris, which Parisian pastry chefs love to replicate in their own way.

•

Preparation time:
45 minutes
Resting time:
15 minutes
Cooking time:
1 hour

•

EQUIPMENT

4-inch (10-cm) square loaf tin

Montmartre cobblestone

INGREDIENTS TO MAKE 1 CAKE

5¾oz (165g) eggs
1 cup plus 1 tbsp (7½oz/215g) superfine (caster) sugar
½ tsp (3g) salt
1 tsp (2g) finely grated lemon zest
Liquid vanilla flavoring
1 cup less 2 tbsp (3¼oz/92g) thick crème fraîche
5¾oz (165g) all-purpose (plain) flour
½ tsp (3g) baking powder
¼ cup (2oz/60g) butter
2 tbsp (1fl oz/30ml) rum
½ cup (2oz/60g) poppy seeds, plus extra for decoration
⅓ cup (3½oz/100g) apricot jam
Butter and flour for the baking frame

Fit a stand mixer with the whisk attachment and lightly whisk together the eggs, sugar, salt, lemon zest, and a few drops of vanilla flavoring. Add the crème fraîche and mix in.

Sift the flour and baking powder together, then whisk into the batter.

Melt the butter in a saucepan or microwave, add the rum, then pour into the batter a little at a time. Add the poppy seeds and whisk everything together. Leave the batter to rest for 15 minutes.

Preheat the oven to 350°F (180°C/Gas mark 4).

Place the baking frame on a baking sheet lined with parchment paper. Butter and flour the baking frame. Pour the batter into the frame and bake for about 1 hour. Remove the frame once the cake has cooled.

Heat the apricot jam with a little water in a saucepan over a medium heat until the mixture simmers. Brush the jam over the cake and coat with poppy seeds.

Le Sabot rouge

This 100 per cent chocolate dessert cake, which is flourless and therefore gluten free, resulted from a meeting I had with Aristide, a Cameroonian cocoa producer; it was thanks to the *Chocolatiers Engagés* initiative that I was able to visit his plantation. I am proud to be part of this association, which has set itself the challenge of changing the rules of the Cameroonian cocoa trade by ensuring an adequate standard of living for producers, while, at the same time, producing quality cocoa in a way that respects the environment.

100%

•

Preparation time:
25 minutes
Chilling time:
1 hour
Cooking time:
25 to 35 minutes

•

EQUIPMENT

4½ x 9½-inch (12 × 24-cm) rectangular baking frame

INGREDIENTS TO SERVE 8

Flourless sponge 2½oz (70g) egg whites • 5⅔ tbsp (2½oz/70g) superfine (caster) sugar • ¼ cup (¾oz/20g) ground almonds • ¼ cup (¾oz/20g) unsweetened cocoa powder • 1¾oz (50g) egg yolks

Chocolate crisp ½ cup (1½oz/45g) ground almonds • 4¾ tbsp (1½oz/40g) all-purpose (plain) flour • 3 tbsp (35g) superfine (caster) sugar • 1¼ tbsp (⅓oz/10g) unsweetened cocoa powder • 1 pinch of salt • 1 pinch of baking powder • 3 tbsp (1½oz/42g) butter, diced • 1¼oz (35g) Artistide couverture chocolate (or another bittersweet/dark chocolate with 70% cacao) • 1¼oz (35g) feuillantine, chopped

Chocolate mousse ½ tsp (1.5g) powdered gelatin • 2 tsp (⅓fl oz/9ml) cold water • 5 tbsp (2½fl oz/75ml) whole milk • 3¾oz (110g) Artistide couverture chocolate (or another bittersweet/dark chocolate with 70% cacao), chopped • ½ cup plus 1½ tbsp (4¾fl oz/145ml) whipping cream

Make the flourless sponge

Preheat the oven to 375°F (190°C/Gas mark 5).

Whisk the egg whites with the sugar until standing in firm peaks. Sift the ground almonds and cocoa together. Using a flexible spatula, gently fold in the egg yolks and sifted almonds and cocoa. Line a baking sheet with parchment paper and place the baking frame on it. Using a spatula, spread the batter into the frame. Bake for 5 to 10 minutes until the sponge is cooked but still soft.

Make the chocolate crisp

Lower the oven temperature to 300°F (150°C/Gas mark 2). Fit a stand mixer with the flat beater attachment, add the dry ingredients and the butter, and mix until like breadcrumbs. Line a baking sheet with parchment paper and spread the mixture over it in a layer about ¾ inch (2cm) thick. Bake for 20 to 25 minutes. Leave to go cold, then transfer to the mixer bowl and reduce to a crumble texture. Melt the chocolate and add to the crumble, along with the feuillantine, mixing all the ingredients together.Spread the crisp over the sponge in an even layer, without removing from the baking frame.

Make the chocolate mousse

Soak the gelatin in the cold water to rehydrate it. Heat the milk in a saucepan, then add the soaked gelatin. Pour the hot milk over the chocolate, mixing to make a ganache. Leave to cool. Once the ganache has cooled to around 77°F (25°C), whip the cream and fold in using a flexible spatula.

Assemble

Turn the sponge layer topped with the chocolate crisp over, still leaving it in the frame. Spoon over the mousse, smoothing the surface with a spatula. Chill in the refrigerator for 1 hour before removing the frame.

If you wish, you can decorate the cake further, or simply dust it with cocoa powder or ice it.

LA CREMAILLERE
"LA CRÉMAILLERE 1900"
RESTAURANT
CABARET
LA CREMAILLERE 1900
RESTAURANT

LA BONNE
FRANQUETTE
Aimer,
Manger,
Boire
et Chanter

Condorcet

Every day I encounter the legacy of the 18th-century French mathematician and philosopher Nicolas de Condorcet in the many places of learning in my neighborhood.

Preparation time:
2 hours
Cooking time:
10 to 12 minutes

EQUIPMENT

8½-inch (22-cm) stainless steel cake ring, 1½ inches (4cm) high

INGREDIENTS TO SERVE 8

Japanese sponge 2 tbsp plus 1 tsp (1¼fl oz/35ml) whole milk · 1 tbsp plus 2 tsp (1oz/25g) butter · 4¼ tbsp (1¼fl oz/35g) all-purpose (plain) flour · 1¼oz (35g) whole eggs · 1¼oz (35g) egg yolks · 2½oz (70g) egg whites · 3½ tbsp (1½/45g) superfine (caster) sugar · 1oz (30g) pistachios, chopped

Morello cherry insert ⅓oz (10g) powdered gelatin · ¼ cup (2fl oz/60ml) cold water · 11oz (310g) morello cherry purée · 3oz (85g) morello cherries · 6¾ tbsp (2oz/60g) powdered (icing) sugar

Pistachio bavarois ¾ cup plus 3 tbsp (210ml) whole milk · 2½ tbsp (1oz/30g) superfine (caster) sugar · 2½oz (75g) egg yolks · 2oz (60g) pistachio paste · 1½ tsp (5g) powdered gelatin · 2 tbsp cold water · 1 cup less 2 tsp (7¾fl oz/230ml) whipping cream (35% fat)

For decoration (optional) Green chocolate spray · 3 cherry halves

Make the Japanese sponge

Preheat the oven to 350°F (180°C/Gas mark 4).

Bring the milk and butter to the boil in a saucepan over a medium heat. Once boiling, take off the heat and add all the flour in one go, mixing for 1 to 2 minutes. Beat together the whole eggs and egg yolks and add. In a bowl, whisk the egg whites until standing in firm peaks, then whisk in the sugar in two or three batches. Combine the two mixtures, folding them gently together using a flexible spatula.

Line a baking sheet with parchment paper and spread the cake batter over it in a 8-inch (20-cm) round and also in a 1½-inch (4-cm) wide band that is long enough to line the internal side of the cake ring. Dust the band with the chopped pistachios.

Bake for 10 to 12 minutes. When the cake comes out of the oven, transfer it to a wire rack to cool.

Make the morello cherry insert

Soak the gelatin in the water to rehydrate it.

Gently heat the morello cherry purée, the morello cherries, and the sugar, stirring until the sugar has dissolved. Add the gelatin and stir it in. Pour onto a flat plate 7 inches (18cm) in diameter and place in the freezer.

Make the pistachio bavarois

Heat the milk in a saucepan over low heat. Whisk the sugar and egg yolks in a mixing bowl.

When the milk boils, pour some of it over the whisked yolks and sugar, stir to mix, and then pour back into the saucepan. Heat until the temperature of the custard reaches 180°F (82°C), stirring continuously with a wooden spatula. Transfer to a bowl, add the pistachio paste, and whisk it in. Soak the gelatin in the cold water to rehydrate it, then add it to the warm custard, stirring until it melts.

Whip the cream. Once the pistachio mixture has cooled to 68°F (20°C), fold in the whipped cream.

Place the baking ring on a board or baking sheet that can go into the refrigerator. Place the sponge round in the ring, then fit the band of pistachio sponge around the side, with the pistachios facing outwards. Pour in some of the pistachio bavarois and spread over the base, then top with the cherry insert, and cover with the remaining bavarois. Smooth the top with a spatula and keep in the refrigerator.

To decorate, I would suggest you buy an aerosol can of green chocolate spray and coat the top of the Condorcet with it, arranging the cherry halves on top.

RUE
SAINT
VINCENT

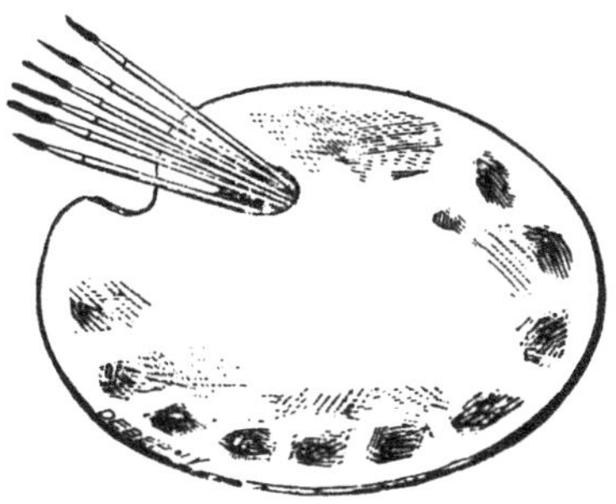

Preparation time:
2 hours
Freezing time:
2 hours
Cooking time:
10 to 15 minutes

EQUIPMENT

8½-inch (22-cm) baking ring, 1¾ inches (4.5cm) high

Gauguin

Before becoming known as the painter of Polynesia, Paul Gauguin lived in the 9th arrondissement. He was born in 1848 at 56 rue Notre-Dame-de-Lorette, very close to Eugène Delacroix. This dessert cake has the sweetness of the Pacific islands.

INGREDIENTS TO SERVE 8

Hazelnut dacquoise sponge

- 2oz (60g) ground hazelnuts
- 1 cup less 1 tbsp (4¾oz/130g) powdered (icing) sugar
- 1¾ tbsp (½oz/15g) all-purpose (plain) flour
- 2¾oz (80g) egg whites
- 5 tbsp (2oz/60g) superfine (caster) sugar

Soft caramel

- ¼ cup (1¾oz/50g) superfine (caster) sugar
- 3 tbsp (1¾oz/50g) liquid glucose
- ½ cup (4fl oz/125ml) whipping cream (35% fat)
- ½ tsp (1.6g) powdered gelatin
- 2 tsp water
- 2 tbsp (1oz/30g) lightly salted butter, diced

Make the hazelnut dacquoise

Preheat the oven to 350°F (180°C/Gas mark 4).

Mix together the ground hazelnuts, powdered sugar, and flour.

Fit a stand mixer with the whisk attachment and whisk the egg whites until standing in firm peaks, adding the sugar in two or three batches. Fold the dry ingredients into the egg whites using a flexible spatula.

Line a large baking sheet with parchment paper. Spoon the batter into a piping bag fitted with a ½-inch (12-mm) plain tip and pipe two rounds, 8½ inches (22cm) in diameter, onto the lined baking sheet. Bake for 10 to 15 minutes until the sponge is cooked but still soft. When the sponge rounds come out of the oven, transfer them to a wire rack to cool.

Make the soft caramel

Heat the sugar and liquid glucose in a saucepan over a medium heat until the mixture becomes a golden brown caramel. Heat the cream in another saucepan, also over a medium heat. Add the hot cream to the caramel and stir in. Soak the gelatin in the cold water to rehydrate it, then melt into the hot caramel. Next add the butter. Leave to cool, then store in the refrigerator.

Recipe continues on next page

Milk chocolate mousse

½ cup less 1 tbsp (3½fl oz/105ml) whole milk

5¾oz (160g) milk melting chocolate (such as Jivara Valrhona®), chopped

¾ tsp (2.5g) powdered gelatin

1 tbsp water

¾ cup plus 3 tbsp (7½fl oz/210ml) whipping cream (35% fat)

Roasted hazelnuts

3½oz (100g) hazelnuts

Chocolate icing

6 tbsp (3fl oz/90ml) water

3 tbsp (1¼oz/35g) superfine (caster) sugar

3 tbsp (1½fl oz/40ml) whipping cream (35% fat)

1½ tbsp (¾oz/20g) liquid glucose

½ tsp (1.5g) pectin NH

5½oz (150g) milk melting chocolate (such as Jivara Valrhona®), chopped

Make the milk chocolate mousse

Bring the milk to the boil in a saucepan over a medium heat, then add the chopped milk chocolate.

Soak the gelatin in the water to rehydrate it and whisk this into the chocolate mixture. Whip the cream. When the temperature of the chocolate mixture is 77°F (25°C), gently mix in the whipped cream with a whisk.

Roast the hazelnuts

Preheat the oven to 325°F (160°C/Gas mark 3). Spread the hazelnuts over a baking sheet and roast them for 5 to 10 minutes. When they come out of the oven, rub them with a dish towel to remove the skins, being careful not to burn your hands.

Make the chocolate icing

Heat 2 tbsp (1oz/30ml) of the water and the sugar in a saucepan to make a syrup. Add the cream, remaining water, and liquid glucose. When the temperature reaches 113°F (45°C), add the pectin and bring to the boil. Pour the hot mixture over the chopped chocolate, stirring until smooth.

Assemble

Place the baking ring on a flat plate or baking sheet and place a sponge round in it. Spoon the soft caramel into a piping bag fitted with a ½-inch (12-mm) plain tip and pipe the caramel over the sponge in concentric circles to within ½-inch (1cm) of the edge. Sprinkle with the whole roasted hazelnuts, reserving a few for the decoration on top. Cover with milk chocolate mousse to the top of the ring, smoothing the top with a spatula. Freeze for 2 hours.

Once the dessert is set, transfer it to a wire rack set over a soup plate or bowl. Drizzle the chocolate icing over it, removing any excess with a spatula. Decorate with the reserved toasted hazelnuts, halved. Transfer to a cake board and chill until your guests arrive.

You will have a second hazelnut sponge round left over that you can freeze to use for another recipe.

The idea for this cake came about after I met Fanny Bouton, the queen of computer geeks. We were immediately imagining what the perfect "gastronogeek" snack would be. We came up with not just Kawaii, but also Dotsie (Opera flavored with raspberry), and Hackaton (chocolate ganache, chocolate cookie, and caramelized pecans).

Kawaii

Preparation time:
2 hours
Freezing time:
At least 3 hours
Cooking time:
30 minutes

EQUIPMENT

8-inch (20-cm) half sphere baking mold

INGREDIENTS
TO SERVE 6 TO 8

Hazelnut sponge

1oz (30g) ground hazelnuts
1oz (30g) ground almonds
⅔ cup (3¼oz/90g) powdered (icing) sugar
4¼oz (120g) egg whites
2½ tbsp (1oz/30g) superfine (caster) sugar

Caramel

3 tbsp (2¼oz/35g) superfine (caster) sugar
2 tbsp (2¼oz/35g) honey or liquid glucose
6 tbsp (3¼fl oz/95ml) whipping cream (35% fat)
¼ tsp (1g) powdered gelatin
1 tsp water
2 tbsp (2oz/30g) butter, diced

Make the hazelnut sponge

Preheat the oven to 325°F (160°C/Gas mark 3). Line a baking sheet with parchment paper.

Sift together the ground hazelnuts and almonds and then the powdered sugar.

Whisk the egg whites in a mixing bowl using an electric hand beater, adding the superfine sugar in two or three batches. Add the sifted ingredients to the egg whites and fold them in with a flexible spatula. Spoon the batter into a piping bag fitted with a ½-inch (12-mm) plain tip, and pipe two rounds, one 4½ inches (12cm) in diameter and the other 7 inches (18cm) in diameter, onto the prepared baking sheet. Bake for 10 to 12 minutes.

Make the caramel

Heat the sugar and liquid glucose or honey in a saucepan over a medium heat, and cook until caramel colored. Warm the cream in another saucepan, then pour it into the caramel and stir until the two are combined.

Soak the gelatin in the water to rehydrate it, then stir it into the caramel. When the temperature of the caramel is around 104°F (40°C), add the butter and mix in. Once cold, chill in the refrigerator until needed.

Recipe continues on next page

Roasted hazelnuts

1oz (30g) whole hazelnuts

Yuzu mousse

7 tbsp (3½fl oz/100ml) yuzu juice
½ cup (3½oz/100g) superfine (caster) sugar
7oz (200g) eggs
5½oz (150g) white chocolate, chopped
1½ tsp (6g) powdered gelatin
2 tbsp plus 1 tsp (1¼fl oz/36ml) cold water
3 tbsp (1½oz/40g) butter, diced
1¼ cups less 1½ tbsp (10fl oz/280ml) whipping cream (35% fat)

White chocolate icing

⅓oz (9g) gelatin leaves
5 tbsp (2½fl oz/75ml) water
¾ cup (5½oz/150g) superfine (caster) sugar
5½oz (150g) liquid glucose
7 tbsp (3½fl oz/100ml) whipping cream (35% fat)
5½oz (150g) white chocolate, chopped

For decoration

Black food coloring
Sugarpaste flowers (see opposite)

Roast the hazelnuts

If you did not leave the oven switched on, preheat it again to 325°F (160°C/Gas mark 3). Spread out the hazelnuts on a baking sheet and roast them for 5 to 10 minutes.

Make the yuzu mousse

Heat the yuzu juice in a saucepan over a medium heat. Whisk the sugar and eggs in a mixing bowl until pale and thickened. When the juice comes to the boil, whisk it into the sugar and egg mixture until combined, then pour the mixture back into the saucepan. Cook, as for a custard, until the temperature reaches 82°F (28°C). Transfer to a mixing bowl and whisk in the chopped white chocolate. Soak the gelatin in the water to rehydrate, then add to the custard. Add the diced butter. Mix well, preferably using an upright blender, until smooth. Whip the cream, then when the temperature of the yuzu cream reaches 68 to 77°F (20 to 25°C), add the whipped cream, mixing it in with a whisk.

Make the white chocolate icing

Soak the gelatin leaves in a bowl of cold water. Put the measured water, sugar, liquid glucose, and cream in a saucepan and bring to the boil (to a temperature of 221°F/105°C). Pour the hot mixture over the chopped chocolate. Squeeze out the gelatin leaves and stir in until dissolved, then leave the icing to cool.

Assemble

Using an offset spatula, spread the caramel over the larger sponge round, taking it right to the edges. Sprinkle it with roasted hazelnuts. Place a ramekin on the work surface and the half sphere mold on it. Half-fill the mold with yuzu mousse. Cover it with the small sponge round, top with the rest of the yuzu mousse, and place the large sponge round on top, with the side sprinkled with hazelnuts and caramel against the mousse. Neaten the mousse around the edges. Freeze the dessert for at least 3 hours. Once frozen, dip the mold in hot water, and turn out onto a wire rack, rounded side up, with a plate underneath. Coat with the white chocolate icing.

Decorate

Once the icing is firmly set, paint the trunk and branches of a cherry tree over it using a brush and black food coloring. Add blossoms made of pastillage.

Made of sugar, starch, and gum, *pastillage* is a modelling icing used for making decorations—and not intended to be eaten—that has been used in pâtisserie work since the 15th century. In the 18th century, when the fashion was for ornamentation, confectioners competed with each other to display their skill and creativity in the art of *pastillage*. Desforges, "first Court decorator" created magnificent cakes for Louis XV. After that, Delorme demonstrated his liking for much sought-after floral arrangements, earning himself the nickname of "Court Florist". Statuettes, animals, plants, often very large: the imagination of pastry chefs and confectioners knew no bounds! Duval, one of the giants who distinguished himself in monumental, colorful *pastillage*, was "confectioner of the king and the small pleasures of Monsieur", owned *Le Grand Monarque* on the rue des Lombards. In 1815, in *Le pâtissier pittoresque*, Antonin Carême cataloged recipes and sketches of these decorative architectural pieces.

Pastillage

PASTILLAGE CAN BE USED FOR MAKING ALL KINDS OF DECORATIONS, VERY OFTEN FLOWERS.

•

Preparation time:
15 minutes

•

INGREDIENTS
TO MAKE 1LB 2OZ (500G) PASTILLAGE

2 gelatin leaves
3 cups (14oz/400g) powdered (icing) sugar
7 tbsp (3½fl oz/100ml) white vinegar
Food coloring, of your choice

Soak the gelatin leaves in a bowl of cold water. Weigh out the powdered sugar and sift it into a mixing bowl.

Once the gelatin is rehydrated, squeeze the leaves to remove excess water, and place them in a mixing bowl. Melt the gelatin in a microwave or water-bath. Add the vinegar and food coloring, mix, and then using a spatula, incorporate the powdered sugar. Finish working the ingredients together by hand until you have a stiff, smooth paste.

Roll out in small quantities, keeping the rest tightly wrapped in plastic wrap (cling film), as it dries out quickly and becomes hard. Cut out different shapes using pastry cutters. Leave to dry flat or draped over molds so they dry in different shapes. These decorations keep well in an airtight container.

Saint-Denis

1

Maisons-Lafitte

2

3

Saint-Germain-en-Laye

8

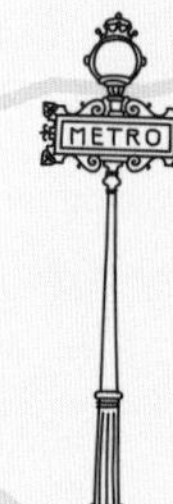

7

6

9

5

11

10

12

4

Versailles

1 —— Talmouse
2 —— Paris–Brest
3 —— Mazarin
Saint-Germain
4 —— Puits d'amour
5 —— Concorde
Succès
Barquettes aux marrons
Fraisier

6 —— Breton cake
7 —— Parisian brioche
8 —— Palmiers
9 —— Sacristains
10 —— Allumettes
11 —— Galette des rois
12 —— Macarons

Greater Paris

Paris has always pushed back its boundaries, gradually spreading its hustle and bustle into the suburbs and broadcasting its creativity at world fairs held in the Champ-de-Mars. Today, the beacon of the Eiffel Tower sheds its light way beyond the boulevards des Maréchaux. Whether in Saint-Denis or Saint-Germain-en-Laye, pâtisserie was already heralding the beginnings of a Greater Paris. While it is sometimes hard to pinpoint the exact origins of certain Parisian cakes, this is perhaps because the city draws pastry chefs from all over the world, blurring the lines of pâtisserie's heritage. As long as something tastes good and looks beautiful, Paris will adapt anything that isn't Parisian in order to make it its own.

The star of street food and popular with residents of the Île-de-France and tourists alike, the talmouse is said to have been the guilty pleasure of Louis XI. A "*talmelier*" was the word in medieval French for a baker and recipes for making talmouse were carefully recorded in 19th century cookery books. Men of letters such as Musset, Dumas, and Balzac praised these little pastry puffs in the shape of a three-cornered hat. Antonin Carême made them with puff pastry filled with Neufchâtel cheese, frangipane, or cream and sugar, and served them at the tables of the Parisian nobility. As to the talmouse's geographical roots, most sources cite the town on the outskirts of Paris but, more Parisian than the Parisians, some enthusiasts believe it was born in the rue Saint-Denis.

Talmouse

•

Preparation time:
45 minutes
Cooking time:
30 minutes

•

EQUIPMENT

5½-inch (14-cm) plain round pastry cutter

INGREDIENTS FOR 8 TALMOUSES

1lb 5oz (600g) puff pastry (see page 230) · 1 egg, beaten, to glaze

Bechamel sauce

3½ tbsp (1¾oz/50g) butter · 6 tbsp (1¾oz/50g) all-purpose (plain) flour · 2 cups (17fl oz/500ml) whole milk · 7oz (200g) Emmental cheese, grated · 1 egg yolk · Freshly grated nutmeg, salt, and pepper

Make the bechamel sauce

First make a roux. Melt the butter in a saucepan, add the flour, and stir into the butter until smooth. Heat the milk in another saucepan until simmering. Gradually add it to the roux, stirring in each addition with a spatula before adding the next. Leave to cook until the sauce thickens; this will take 5 to 10 minutes over a medium heat.

Season the sauce with nutmeg, salt, and pepper. Add the grated Emmental and egg yolk, and mix in. Set aside to cool, then chill.

Assemble the talmouses

Preheat the oven to 350°F (180°C/Gas mark 4).

Roll out the puff pastry ⅛ inch (3mm) thick. Using the pastry cutter, cut out eight rounds. Break the egg into a ramekin and beat. Brush the egg over the puff pastry rounds and spoon or pipe bechamel sauce into the middle of each round. Shape each into a triangle by folding the edges toward the center and pressing them together to fix them securely in place. Each one needs to be a well-sealed three-pointed turnover.

Line a baking sheet with parchment paper and place the talmouses on it. Brush them twice with the beaten egg to glaze. Bake for 30 minutes.

Eat hot, or cold with a salad.

Vincent La Chapelle, a chef inspired by the Age of Enlightenment, shocked prudish minds first in England and later in France with his metaphorical, but no less erotic *puits d'amour* (wells of love). In 1733, he published a recipe for them in English in *The Modern Cook*, where they bore a striking resemblance to *vol-au-vents* filled rather suggestively with red fruit jam, and then nine years later in French in *Le Cuisinier Moderne*. Shocking indeed!

Preparation time:
1 hour
Chilling time:
3 hours
Cooking time:
15 minutes

EQUIPMENT

2½-inch (6-cm) plain round pastry cutter
1½-inch (4-cm) plain round pastry cutter
Chef's blowtorch

Puits d'amour

INGREDIENTS
TO MAKE 6 PUITS D'AMOUR

1lb 2oz (500g) puff pastry (see page 230)
1 egg beaten, to glaze
½ cup (3½oz/100g) brown sugar

Crème pâtissière

1 cup (8fl oz/240ml) milk
5 tbsp (2oz/60g) sugar
1oz (25g) egg
¾oz (20g) egg yolk
Natural vanilla flavoring, to taste
¼ cup (1oz/25g) cornstarch (cornflour)

Roll out the puff pastry ⅛ inch (3mm) thick. Using the larger pastry cutter, cut out 12 puff pastry rounds.

Line a baking sheet with parchment paper and place six of the rounds on it. Brush the beaten egg over the rounds to glaze them.

Using the smaller pastry cutter, cut out the centers of the six remaining pastry rounds to make rings. Lay the rings on top of the six larger rounds and brush them with beaten egg as well to glaze. Chill in the refrigerator for 3 hours.

Toward the end of the chilling time, preheat the oven to 425°F (220°C/Gas mark 7). Bake the pastry cases for 15 minutes and leave to cool on a wire rack.

Make the crème pâtissière

Bring the milk and half the sugar to the boil in a saucepan.

Whisk the whole egg, egg yolk, the rest of the sugar, and the vanilla in a mixing bowl until pale and thickened. Sift in the cornstarch and mix in. Pour in half the boiling milk, whisk to combine, then pour the mixture back into the saucepan. Stir constantly for 2 to 3 minutes until boiling and the mixture has the consistency of a custard.

When ready to fill the pastry cases, whisk the crème pâtissière to loosen it. Spoon it into a piping bag fitted with a ½-inch (12-mm) plain tip and fill the cases with it. Sprinkle brown sugar over the top of the pastry cases and caramelize with a chef's blowtorch, repeating this twice.

Parisian brioche

Preparation time:
20 minutes
Resting and rising time:
6 hours 15 minutes
Cooking time:
10 to 15 minutes (for the small brioche)
25 to 30 minutes (for the large brioche)

•

EQUIPMENT

7 small brioche molds or 1 large brioche mold

•

INGREDIENTS
TO MAKE 7 SMALL OR 1 LARGE BRIOCHE

1¾ cups plus 2 tbsp (9oz/250g) all-purpose (plain) flour, plus extra for shaping
5oz (145g) whole eggs, plus 1 egg, beaten, to glaze
2 tbsp (1oz/25g) superfine (caster) sugar
1¼ tsp (5g) salt
⅓oz (10g) baker's (fresh) yeast
⅔ cup less 1 tsp (5oz/145g) butter, diced and softened
Butter for the mold(s)

Place all the ingredients, except the butter, in the bowl of a stand mixer fitted with the dough hook attachment, making sure the yeast does not come into contact with the sugar and salt.

Knead for 5 minutes on the lowest speed, then increase the speed to the next level and knead for a further 10 to 15 minutes. Scrape down the sides of the bowl and then incorporate the butter, a little at a time.

Knead for a further 5 minutes on the same speed until the dough detaches itself from the sides of the bowl and is smooth, shiny, and elastic. Cover the dough with plastic wrap (cling film) and leave to rest for 30 minutes at room temperature.

Fold the dough over to expel as much air as possible. Re-cover with plastic wrap and chill in the refrigerator for 4 hours.

Using a dough cutter, divide the dough into seven balls, each weighing 2½oz (70g) for small brioche or, if making one large brioche, one 12¾oz (360g) ball for the body and three 2½oz (70g) balls for the head.

To make seven small brioches

Butter the molds. Roll the 2½oz (70g) pieces of dough into balls and leave to rest for 15 minutes in the refrigerator. Roll each dough ball into a small sausage. Using the side of your hand, press the dough lightly about two-thirds of the way along to mark a "throat", separating the head from the body.

Dip three fingers in flour and, holding the brioche "head", place the dough in the mold, pushing your fingers all the way to the bottom. With one finger, work your way around the head, again pushing all the way to the bottom of the mold to ensure the head is centered and sealed firmly to the body. Repeat with the remaining six balls of dough.

Leave the brioches to rise at a temperature of 79°F (26°C) for 1 hour 30 minutes. When they have risen, preheat the oven to 400°F (200°C/Gas mark 6). Brush the brioche with beaten egg to glaze and bake for 10 to 15 minutes. Unmold them when they come out of the oven.

To make one large brioche

Butter the mold. Roll the large piece of dough into a ball and, using your thumb, pinch and widen the center, stretching the dough to form a "life belt". Press your thumb, index, and middle fingers together and push them into the dough to make a large doughnut-shaped cavity. Place it in the bottom of the buttered mold.

Roll one small ball into a pear shape and push the thin end into the hole in the main dough. Dip your fingers in flour and press all around to form a smooth, round head. Leave the brioche to rise at a temperature of 79°F (26°C) for 1 hour 30 minutes.

When risen, preheat the oven to 350°F (180°C/Gas mark 4). Brush the brioche with beaten egg to glaze and bake for 25 to 30 minutes.

Unmold the brioche when it comes out of the oven. The two remaining small balls of dough can be made into two small brioche.

Found in any bakery or pâtisserie in France, the *palmier* ("palm tree" in English) owes its name to its plant-like shape, but this classic treat is known around the world by a variety of other things it resembles, including *oreilles* (ears), *coeurs* (hearts), and *lunettes* (spectacles).

Palmiers

Preparation time:
2 hours 30 minutes
Chilling time:
12 hours + 4 hours + 4 hours
Cooking time:
15 to 20 minutes

INGREDIENTS TO MAKE 10 PALMIERS

¾ cup (6fl oz/180ml) water
2½ tsp (⅓oz/10g) salt
¼ cup (2oz/60g) butter, melted and cooled
2½ cups less 1½ tbsp (11¼oz/315g) T55 flour
¾ cup plus 1 tsp (3½oz/105g) all-purpose (plain) flour, plus extra for rolling out
1½ cups (11¾oz/335g) butter, in one block for laminating
1½ cups (10½oz/300g) granulated sugar

Mix the water and salt with the melted and cooled butter. Put the mixture in the bowl of a stand mixer fitted with the dough hook attachment, add the flours and mix on the lowest speed. Stop when the ingredients are combined. Cover the dough with plastic wrap (cling film) and chill in the refrigerator for 12 hours.

Roll out the dough to a 10-inch (25-cm) square. Flatten the laminating butter with the rolling pin and place it in the centre of the dough. Wrap the four corners of the dough toward the center to enclose the butter like a square envelope.

Roll out the dough on a lightly floured surface to a rectangle three times as long as it is wide. Fold the dough in three and repeat the rolling and folding once more, having given the dough two turns. Cover the dough in plastic wrap and chill it in the refrigerator for 4 hours.

Roll and fold the dough twice more to give it four turns, not forgetting to dust the work surface lightly with flour each time. Wrap and chill the dough for a further 4 hours, then repeat the rolling and folding, replacing the flour on the work surface with granulated sugar. The dough will have had six turns in total. As you roll the dough over the sugar, it is a good idea to apply light pressure on the rolling pin so that the sugar gets pressed into the pastry.

Next, roll the dough to a rectangle measuring about 12 x 32 inches (30 × 80cm). Fold the two long sides toward the center, overlapping them slightly. Fold over again in the same way, making sure the edges of the dough overlap. Using the rolling pin, lightly press on the top to lengthen the dough and then fold it in two.

Cut the log of dough into slices about ½ inch (1cm) thick. Line a baking sheet with parchment paper and place the slices flat on it, making sure to leave plenty of space between them.

Preheat the oven to 400°F (200°C/Gas mark 6). Bake the palmiers for 15 to 20 minutes. For the best caramelization, turn the slices over half way through the cooking time.

The only connection to Paris this cake has is that it was unveiled at the 1867 Paris World Fair when the recipe for it was officially recognized. The Breton cake was actually developed by a Swiss pastry chef called Crucer, who was married to a Breton woman from Lorient. It proves that pâtisserie knows no boundaries!

•

Preparation time:
15 minutes
Chilling time:
30 minutes
Cooking time:
40 to 45 minutes

•

EQUIPMENT

8-inch (20-cm) round cake pan

Breton cake

INGREDIENTS
TO SERVE 6 TO 8

1 cup (7oz/200g) superfine (caster) sugar
1 cup plus 2 tbsp (9oz/250g) butter, diced, at room temperature
2¼ cups (10½oz/300g) T55 flour, plus extra for rolling out (optional)
A pinch of salt
3½oz (100g) egg yolks
1 egg beaten, to glaze

Fit a stand mixer with the flat beater attachment and beat the sugar, butter, flour, and salt together until crumbly. Add the egg yolks and beat again until smooth. Cover in plastic wrap (cling film) and chill the dough in the refrigerator for 30 minutes.

Roll out the dough to an 8-inch (20-cm) round and place it in the cake pan. You can dust the work surface with 1oz (25g) flour if you wish, to make rolling out easier. Brush the dough twice with the beaten egg to glaze and, using a fork, score a criss-cross pattern on top.

Preheat the oven to 325°F (170°C/Gas mark 3). Bake the cake for 40 to 45 minutes. When it comes out of the oven, turn the cake out onto a wire rack to cool.

In their most basic form, these sweet almond pastries have been around since the Middle Ages. Shaped like small sticks, they represent the canes carried by sacristans, officers whose responsibility it was to look after churches and their contents.

Sacristains

Preparation time: 20 minutes
Cooking time: 10 to 15 minutes

INGREDIENTS
TO MAKE ABOUT 20 SACRISTAINS

1lb 2oz (500g) puff pastry (see page 230)
1 egg beaten, to glaze
1 cup less 1½ tbsp (6¼oz/180g) granulated sugar
6¼oz (180g) chopped almonds

Preheat the oven to 400°F (200°C/Gas mark 6).

Roll out the puff pastry into a 8¼-inch (21-cm) square, ⅛ inch (3mm) thick. Brush with beaten egg to glaze. Sprinkle the sugar over one half and the chopped almonds over the other half. Press lightly over the top with the rolling the pin to ensure the sugar and almonds stick to the pastry.

Turn the pastry square over. Brush the other side with the beaten egg and sprinkle one half with the remaining sugar and the other with the remaining chopped almonds. Roll the pin lightly over the top.

Line a baking sheet with parchment paper. Cut the pastry into 21 strips, each measuring 8¼ x ½ in (21 × 1cm). Twist each strip twice into a spiral and place them on the baking sheet, spacing them apart.

Bake for 10 to 15 minutes.

In 1840 the Swiss pastry chef Planta, living in Dinan, gave his name to these pastry sticks, which he decorated by chance with leftover frosting (icing). They are one of the many variations of the puff pastry making technique. If the first written mentions of puff pastry go back to the 16th century, the technique of "tourage" was not developed until the 17th century by the French artist and apprentice baker Claude Gellée, also known as Le Lorrain.

Allumettes

•

Preparation time: 30 minutes
Cooking time: 10 minutes

•

INGREDIENTS TO MAKE 20 ALLUMETTES

9oz (250g) puff pastry (see page 230)

Royal icing

1 egg white (1½oz/40g)

1 ⅔ cups (8oz/225g) powdered (icing) sugar

A few drops of lemon juice

Flaked almonds, for decoration

Make the puff pastry, giving it six turns. Roll out the pastry to ⅛ inch (4mm) thick. Cut into long strips and chill them in the refrigerator.

Preheat the oven to 400°F (200°C/Gas mark 6). Line a baking sheet with parchment paper.

Make the royal icing by lightly whisking the egg white, then gradually whisking in the powdered sugar and lemon juice until smooth. Using a palette knife, spread a thin layer of icing over the puff pastry strips.

Cut the strips into 1½-inch (4-cm) wide slices and decorate the top of each with a flaked almond. Place on the baking sheet.

Bake for about 10 minutes until the top of each allumette is pale cream.

NOTE: SERVE THE ALLUMETTES WITH COFFEE OR TEA. YOU CAN ALSO CUT THEM IN HALF AND FILL THEM WITH WHIPPED CHANTILLY CREAM.

Galette des rois

•
Preparation time:
30 minutes
Chilling time:
30 minutes
+ 12 hours if making the puff pastry
Cooking time:
35 minutes
•

INGREDIENTS TO SERVE 8

1lb 9oz (700g) puff pastry (see page 230 or buy ready-made all-butter puff pastry) • 1 dried bean or food-safe small charm • 1 egg beaten, to glaze

Frangipane filling ⅓ cup less 1 tsp (2½oz/70g) butter, diced • 5⅔ tbsp (2½oz/70g) superfine (caster) sugar • ⅔ cup (2½oz/70g) ground almonds • 2½oz (70g) whole eggs, beaten • 1¾ tbsp (½oz/15g) all-purpose (plain) flour • 1 tbsp rum

Syrup 3½ tbsp (1¾fl oz/50ml) water • ¼ cup (1¾oz/50g) superfine (caster) sugar

Roll out the puff pastry 1/10 inch (2.5mm) thick. Cut out two 11¼-inch (28-cm) rounds and chill in the refrigerator until needed.

Make the frangipane filling

Fit a stand mixer with the flat beater attachment and mix the butter and sugar together on low speed. Add the ground almonds, followed by the eggs, a little at a time. The ingredients must be evenly combined so, if necessary, scrape down the sides of the bowl with a flexible spatula to ensure the mixture is smooth. Finally add the flour and the rum, stirring them in. Set aside at room temperature.

Make the syrup

Heat the water and sugar in a saucepan until the sugar melts, then bring to the boil to make a syrup.

Assemble

Line a baking sheet with parchment paper and place one pastry round on it. Using a pastry brush dipped in cold water, dampen the pastry edges all round. Spoon the frangipane filling into a piping bag fitted with a ½-inch (1-cm) plain tip and pipe it over one of the pastry rounds to within ¾ inch (2cm) of the edge. Press the bean or charm gently into the edge of the filling. Lift and place the second pastry round on top and seal the edge by pressing the two layers of pastry lightly together. Mark a decorative pattern with the back of a paring knife around the edge. Chill in the refrigerator for 30 minutes.

Beat the egg in a ramekin and brush it over the pastry twice to glaze. Lightly score a decorative pattern on top with the blade of a knife, without cutting all the way through the pastry.

Preheat the oven to 375°F (190°C/Gas mark 5) and bake for 35 minutes. When the galette comes out of the oven, brush the syrup over it.

A traditional family dessert, the recipe for which has been passed down through many generations. Should it be described as a kings' cake or a pastry galette? And filled with almond cream or frangipane? Parisians have been eating "puff pastry cakes" since the 16th century and an actual recipe for puff pastry was first mentioned in 1651 by François Pierre de La Varenne in *Le Cuisinier François (The French Cook)* and then again two years later in *Le Pâtissier François (The French Pastry Chef)*. Made by bakers and pastry chefs alike, this very popular sweet treat became the privilege of the latter when in 1718 they obtained exclusive authorization to use eggs, butter, and sugar. Today, everyone can make it for Epiphany!

In the 1970s, the far-sighted Gaston Lenôtre, who was director of catering for Air France, designed this cake as a way of paying tribute to what was a landmark in the history of aviation—the invention of the supersonic Concorde.

Concorde

Preparation time:
50 minutes
Cooking time:
1 hour 30 minutes
Chilling time:
1 hour

INGREDIENTS
TO SERVE 10

Chocolate-flavored French meringue

- ⅓ cup (1¼oz/35g) extra bitter cocoa powder
- 1 cup (5½oz/150g) powdered (icing) sugar
- 5½oz (150g) egg whites
- ¾ cup (5½oz/150g) superfine (caster) sugar

Make the chocolate-flavored French meringue

Preheat the oven to 300°F (150°C/Gas mark 2).

Sift the cocoa powder and powdered sugar together. Whisk the egg whites until standing in firm peaks, whisking in 2 tbsp (¾oz/20g) of the superfine sugar halfway. Once the whites are sufficiently firm, whisk in the remaining superfine sugar a little at a time on low speed, then, using a spatula, quickly fold in the sifted cocoa and powdered sugar.

Line two baking sheets with parchment paper. Spoon about two-thirds of the meringue into a piping bag fitted with a ½-inch (12-mm) plain tip and pipe three ovals, each measuring about 10½ x 5½ inches (26 × 14cm), onto one of the sheets. Spoon the rest of the meringue into another piping bag fitted with a ⅛-inch (3-mm) plain tip and pipe a mixture of wide and narrow strips onto the other sheet, making sure they do not touch.

Bake for 1 hour 50 minutes. It is a good idea to rotate the baking sheets halfway through the baking time to ensure even cooking. If necessary, the three ovals can stay in the oven for 10 minutes more (it must be easy to lift them off the parchment paper).

Recipe continues on next page

Chocolate mousse

6oz (170g) bittersweet (dark) chocolate (70% cacao), chopped

½ cup less 1 tbsp (3½oz/100g) butter, diced and at room temperature

2oz (60g) egg yolks

5¾oz (160g) egg whites

2 tbsp (1oz/25g) superfine (caster) sugar

For decoration

½ cup (2½oz/70g) powdered (icing) sugar

Make the chocolate mousse

Melt the chocolate in a water-bath, then remove from the heat and whisk in the butter.

Whisk in the egg yolks. The temperature must not get too warm, no higher than 68°F to 77°F (20°C to 25°C) or it will be too liquid to be incorporated with the whisked whites.

Whisk the egg whites until standing in firm peaks, adding the superfine sugar halfway. Pour the chocolate mixture over the whisked whites and lightly fold the two together with a flexible spatula.

Assemble

Place one cold meringue layer on a cake board of the same shape and, using a spatula, spread one third of the chocolate mousse over it. Place a second meringue on top, spread with another third of the chocolate mousse, and finish by covering with the last meringue. Spread the top and sides with the rest of the mousse to cover the layered meringues completely.

Cut the meringue strips into 1-inch (2.5-cm) "fairies' fingers" and carefully press them around the sides and over the top of the cake. Chill for 1 hour. Cut a round of cardboard slightly smaller than the top of the cake and place it carefully in the center. Dust the sides of the cake with powdered sugar, leaving the center dark.

IF THERE ARE ANY FAIRIES' FINGERS LEFTOVER, THEY WILL BE EXCELLENT SERVED WITH COFFEE.

The word "macaron" first appeared in 1552 in Rabelais' *Le Quart Livre* (*The Fourth Book*). Since then, macarons have been baked in the French provinces and Italy. In the 19th century, the fashion was to fill the two shells with jam, fruit compote, or buttercream, with the shells reflecting the French taste for almonds. It was a Parisian pastry chef who added the ganache filling. Today, on the international stage, the macaron is the jewel in the crown of French pâtisserie, being made by the great Parisian chefs and houses such as Pierre Hermé and Ladurée.

Macarons

•
Preparation time:
1 hour
Chilling time:
2 to 3 hours
Cooking time:
15 minutes
•

INGREDIENTS TO MAKE 18 MACARONS

Shells 1½ cups (5½oz/150g) ground almonds · 1 cup (5½oz/150g) powdered (icing) sugar · 4¼oz (120g) egg whites · 3 tbsp water · ¾ cup (5½oz/150g) superfine (caster) sugar

Ganache ¾ cup (6fl oz/180ml) whipping cream (35% fat) · 6¼oz (180g) bittersweet (dark) chocolate (70% cacao), chopped · 1 tbsp honey

Make the shells

Mix the ground almonds and powdered sugar together in a mixing bowl. It is a good idea to first grind the ingredients together in a food processor to make an even fine powder, but avoid overprocessing and making the mixture warm. Add 2oz (60g) of the egg whites to the almonds and sugar and mix in with a spatula.

Make an Italian meringue. Heat the water and sugar in a saucepan over a medium heat until the sugar dissolves and the temperature reaches 248°F (120°C).

Whisk the remaining egg whites until they stand in firm peaks. Pour the syrup over the whites in a thin, steady stream, whisking constantly.

Using a flexible spatula, add the Italian meringue to the almond mixture, combining the two, and letting the volume sink a little but not by too much.

Line a baking sheet with a silicone baking mat or parchment paper. Spoon the meringue into a piping bag fitted with a plain tip, and pipe rounds onto the sheet. Tap the underside of the baking sheet lightly on the work surface to smooth the tops of the macaron shells.

Preheat the oven to 300°F (150°C/Gas mark 2) and bake the shells for about 15 minutes. When the shells come out of the oven, leave them to cool.

Make the ganache

Heat the cream in a saucepan over a medium heat. When it comes to the boil, pour it over the chopped chocolate, stirring with a spatula. Add the honey and stir until smooth.

Assemble

Spoon the ganache into a piping bag fitted with a ½-inch (12-mm) plain tip and pipe the ganache onto the flat side of half the shells. Press the flat side of the remaining shells lightly on top.

Chill in the refrigerator for up to 2 or 3 hours before serving.

A name that was destined for one of Gaston Lenôtre's many creations. Known simply as "the pastry chef of the 20th century", his school at Plaisir in the Yvelines, is still training the pastry chefs, confectioners, and cooks of today.

Succès

Preparation time:
1 hour 20 minutes
Cooking time:
45 to 50 minutes

INGREDIENTS TO SERVE 8

Succès layers 5 egg whites • 1 tbsp plus 2 tsp (¾oz/20g) superfine (caster) sugar (1) + ¾ cup plus 1½ tbsp (6oz/170g) superfine (caster) sugar (2) • ⅔ cup (3¼oz/90g) powdered (icing) sugar • Scant 1 cup (3¼oz/90g) ground almonds • 3½ tbsp (1¾fl oz/50ml) whole milk • Butter for the baking sheets

Praline buttercream ⅓ cup (2½fl oz/80ml) water • 1 cup (7oz/200g) superfine (caster) sugar • 8 egg yolks • 1 cup plus 2 tbsp (9oz/250g) butter, diced into small pieces • 3½oz (100g) praline, crushed

To assemble and finish ¾ cup (3½oz/100g) powdered (icing) sugar • 1¾oz (50g) nougatine, crushed

Make the succès layers

Whisk the egg whites until standing in firm peaks, slowly adding the smaller quantity of superfine sugar (1). In a mixing bowl, mix the larger quantity of superfine sugar (2) with the powdered sugar, ground almonds, and milk. Pour a little of the egg white mixture into the almond mixture to loosen, then return it all to the first bowl. Mix together quickly but gently with a spatula.

Cut two pieces of parchment paper each large enough to line a baking sheet. Using a pencil, draw a 7-inch (18-cm) circle on each piece of parchment and use it to line a baking sheet—you can flip it over so that the pencil is underneath, and use a smear of butter to stick it to the baking sheet, if you need to. Spoon the mixture into a piping bag fitted with a ¾-inch (2-cm) plain tip and pipe two tight spirals of mixture to fill the drawn circles, starting in the middle of each and working outwards.

Preheat the oven to 300°F (150°C/Gas mark 2) and bake the shells for 45 to 50 minutes. Take care when baking the succès layers as they can quickly stick. The layers will keep well in an airtight container for several days.

Make the praline buttercream

Heat the water and sugar in a saucepan until the sugar melts and the temperature reaches 248°F (120°C).

Whisk the egg yolks in a bowl (by hand or using an electric beater). When the syrup is ready, pour it from the saucepan over the yolks in a thin, steady, stream and, using an electric hand beater on medium speed, continue whisking until the yolk mixture is completely cold. Whisk in the diced butter until the mixture is smooth. Finally stir in the praline.

Assemble and finish

Reserve the best looking succès layer for the top. Place the other layer on a cake board of the same diameter. Spoon about 1lb 5oz (600g) of the praline buttercream into a piping bag fitted with a plain tip and pipe small mounds all over the layer. Place the second succès layer on top, pressing it down lightly. Using a stainless steel palette knife, spread the remaining buttercream over the top if wished. Dust generously with icing sugar, if wished, and press the crushed nougatine into the buttercream around the sides. Chill in the refrigerator before serving.

Louis Durand, a baker in Maisons-Laffitte, a district on the outskirts of Paris, is credited with creating this cake, which he named after the bicycle race that passed in front of his store. The choux pastry crown represents a bicycle wheel and, while professional champions on two wheels no longer wear out their tyres peddling the Paris–Brest loop since 1951, this sweet dessert has survived!

Paris-Brest

Preparation time:
1 hour 15 minutes
Chilling time:
45 minutes + 30 minutes
Cooling time:
1 hour
Cooking time:
45 minutes

INGREDIENTS TO SERVE 8

1lb 10oz (750g) choux pastry dough (see page 230) · 1¼ cups (3½oz/100g) flaked almonds

Crème pâtissière 1½ cups (12oz/350ml) whole milk · 2oz (60g) egg yolks · 5 ⅔ tbsp (2½oz/70g) superfine (caster) sugar · ¾oz (20g) custard powder · 2 tbsp (15g) cornstarch (cornflour)

Praline mousseline cream 7 tbsp (3¼oz/90g) superfine (caster) sugar · 1½oz (45g) hazelnuts · 1½oz (45g) almonds · ⅔ cup (5½oz/150g) butter, diced and softened

For decoration Powdered (icing) sugar

Make the crème pâtissière

Heat the milk in a saucepan over a medium heat. Whisk the egg yolks with the sugar, custard powder, and cornstarch. Whisk in a little of the hot milk, then pour the mixture back into the saucepan. Whisk constantly over the heat until boiling and the mixture has the consistency of a custard. Cool, then chill in the refrigerator for 45 minutes.

Bake the choux pastry

Preheat the oven to 350°F (180°C/Gas mark 4). Line a baking sheet with parchment paper.

Spoon the choux pastry dough into a piping bag fitted with a ½-inch (12-mm) plain tip and pipe a circle 7 inches (18cm) in diameter on the parchment paper. Pipe a second circle just inside the first and touching it, then a third on top of the join between the first two circles. Dust with the flaked almonds. Pipe a final circle 6¼ inches (16cm) in diameter. Bake for 45 minutes.

Make the praline mousseline cream

Put the sugar, hazelnuts, and almonds in a saucepan over a medium heat. When the sugar has dissolved, continue cooking until the nuts are roasted. Line a baking sheet with parchment paper and tip the nuts onto it. Leave to cool for 1 hour. Chop in a food processor, leaving the motor running until you have a paste, but one that is not oily. Whisk the crème pâtissière until smooth. Add the softened butter and praline and whisk again to make a creamy mousseline.

Assemble

Once the baked choux has cooled, slice it in half horizontally two-thirds of the way up using a serrated knife. Spoon the mousseline cream into a piping bag fitted with a ½-inch (12-mm) fluted tip and pipe the cream over the base of the crown. Place the single choux pastry ring on top and pipe mousseline cream over it to resemble flames. Place the crown on top and dust with powdered sugar. Chill for 30 minutes before serving.

The charismatic Gaston Lenôtre, who trained several generations of today's pastry chefs, created this emblematic recipe, the title of which translates into English as "little chestnut boats".

Barquettes
aux marrons

•
Preparation time:
1 hour 30 minutes
Cooking time:
15 to 20 minutes
•

EQUIPMENT

Oval-shaped boat pastry cutter

12 boat molds

INGREDIENTS TO MAKE 12 BARQUETTES

12¾oz (360g) sweet tart pastry (see page 131) · 14oz (400g) chestnut spread · ½ cup less 1 tbsp (3½oz/100g) softened butter · 20ml syrup (made with 10g sugar, plus 10g water) · 2 tbsp sugarcane juice rum

Almond cream 3 tbsp (45g) butter · ¼ cup less 1 tsp (1½oz/45g) superfine (caster) sugar · Scant ½ cup (1½oz/45g) ground almonds · 1½oz (45g) egg · 3½ tsp (⅓oz/10g) all-purpose (plain) flour · 2 tsp rum · Natural vanilla flavoring, to taste

Rum syrup ¼ cup (1¾oz/50g) superfine (caster) sugar · 3½ tbsp (1¾fl oz/50ml) water · 1 tsp rum

Italian meringue 2 tbsp water · 7 tbsp (3¼oz/90g) superfine (caster) sugar · 1½oz (45g) egg whites

Icing 7½oz (210g) bittersweet (dark) chocolate, chopped · 2 tbsp neutral-flavored oil

Roll out the sweet tart pastry ¹⁄₁₀ inch (2.5mm) thick. Cut out 12 boat shapes using the oval pastry cutter and line the boat molds with them, trimming the edges if necessary.

Make the almond cream

Preheat the oven to 350°F (180°C/Gas mark 4).

Fit a stand mixer with the flat beater attachment and mix the butter and sugar together on low speed. Add the ground almonds and then the egg. Mix until smooth, scraping down the sides of the bowl with a pastry scraper or flexible spatula, if necessary. Next add the flour, rum, and vanilla and mix everything together.

Spoon the mixture into a piping bag fitted with a plain tip and pipe the cream into the pastry cases to half-fill them. Bake for 15 to 20 minutes.

Make the rum syrup

Dissolve the sugar in the water in a saucepan over a medium heat to make a syrup, then add the rum. When the pastry cases come out of the oven, brush them lightly with the rum syrup.

Make the Italian meringue

Heat the water and sugar in a saucepan over medium heat and, when the sugar has dissolved, cook until the temperature of the syrup reaches 240°F (120°C). Meanwhile, whisk the egg whites to firm peaks in a mixing bowl, then pour in the syrup in a thin, steady, stream, whisking until the mixture is cold.

Assemble and ice

Using a spatula, mix the chestnut spread and softened butter together. Whisk in the syrup and rum until the mixture is smooth and soft. Add the Italian meringue and mix in.

Spoon the mixture into a piping bag fitted with a Saint-Honoré tip and pipe five "flames" in each pastry case. Transfer to the freezer until firm but not frozen solid.

Make the icing by melting the chocolate with the oil in a water-bath, taking care not to let the mixture become too hot; the temperature should not rise above 104°F (40°C). Dip the tops of the boats in the icing, leave to cool, and then enjoy!

This strawberry cake became popular in the 20th century although its exact origins remain uncertain. Gaston Lenôtre's bagatelle is one of the modern interpretations.

Fraisier

Preparation time:
2 hours
Chilling time:
1 hour 30 minutes
Cooking time:
20 minutes

EQUIPMENT

12-inch (30-cm) cake ring, 2½ inches (6cm) high

INGREDIENTS
TO SERVE 8

Genoese sponge

2¼oz (65g) almond paste, chopped
6¼oz (180g) eggs, beaten
6 tbsp (2½oz/75g) superfine (caster) sugar
¾ cup (3½oz/100g) all-purpose (plain) flour
3 tbsp (1½oz/40g) butter, melted and still lukewarm
Natural liquid vanilla flavoring

Crème pâtissière

2½ cups (20¼fl oz/580ml) whole milk
½ cup plus 1¼ tbsp (4oz/115g) superfine (caster) sugar
1 vanilla bean, slit lengthwise and seeds scraped out
4oz (115g) eggs
3⅔ tbsp (1oz/30g) all-purpose (plain) flour
⅓ cup (1oz/30g) cornstarch (cornflour)
¼ cup (2oz/60g) butter, diced

Make the Genoese sponge

Fit a stand mixer with the whisk attachment. Place the chopped almond paste in the bowl and gradually whisk in the eggs a little at a time, scraping down the sides of the bowl with a flexible spatula, if necessary, to make a smooth mixture. Once the eggs have been incorporated, add the sugar and beat for a few minutes on medium speed. Add a few drops of vanilla flavoring, then sift in the flour, and finally add the warm melted butter. Mix everything together until smooth.

Preheat the oven to 350°F (180°C/Gas mark 4). Line a baking sheet with a silicone baking mat or parchment paper and place the cake ring on it. Pour the cake batter into the ring and bake for 16 to 18 minutes. When the sponge comes out of the oven, remove the cake ring, and leave the Genoese to cool on a wire rack.

Make the crème pâtissière

Heat the milk with half the sugar and the vanilla pod and seeds in a saucepan over a medium heat.

Whisk the eggs with the rest of the sugar in a mixing bowl until pale and thickened. Sift in the flour and cornstarch and fold in. When the milk mixture comes to the boil, pour some of it over the egg mixture to loosen it, then pour back into the saucepan and bring to the boil for 2 to 3 minutes, stirring constantly and briskly. Remove the pan from the heat and mix in the butter. Spread the crème pâtissière in a shallow tray, cover it with plastic wrap (cling film), and chill in the refrigerator. (You will need to remove it 30 minutes before you make the mousseline cream.)

Recipe continues on next page

Italian meringue

¾ cup plus 2 tbsp (7fl oz/200ml) water

7 tbsp (2¾oz/80g) superfine (caster) sugar

3½oz (100g) egg whites

Mousseline cream

1⅓ cups plus 1 tbsp (11oz/310g) softened butter

1 tbsp raspberry liqueur

Seeds from 1 vanilla bean

Syrup

1 cup (8fl oz/240ml) water

1¼ cups less 1 tbsp (8½oz/240g) superfine (caster) sugar

2 tbsp raspberry liqueur

To assemble

10½oz (300g) strawberries

5½oz (150g) white almond paste

Make the Italian meringue

Heat the water and sugar in a saucepan over a medium heat and, when the sugar has dissolved, cook until the temperature of the syrup reaches 240°F (120°C). Whisk the egg whites until standing in firm peaks, then whisk in the sugar syrup in a thin, steady, stream. Continue whisking until the meringue and bowl are completely cold.

Make the mousseline cream

Remove the crème pâtissière from the refrigerator 30 minutes before preparing the mousseline cream so it has time to come to room temperature. Using a whisk, mix 2lb 1oz (930g) crème pâtissière with the softened butter, then gently fold in 5½oz (155g) Italian meringue, using a flexible spatula. Add the raspberry liqueur and the vanilla seeds.

Make the syrup

Heat the water and sugar in a saucepan over a medium heat. Once the sugar has dissolved, bring to the boil, then turn off the heat. Leave to cool, then add the raspberry liqueur.

Assemble

Using a serrated knife, cut the Genoese horizontally in half through the center. Place the cake ring on a plate or board and lay one sponge layer in it. Brush lightly with the syrup. Spread half the mousseline cream over the sponge using a spatula.

Wash and hull the strawberries and reserve a few for the top. Arrange the rest of the strawberries over the mousseline cream, placing them tightly together. Cover with the remaining mousseline cream, smoothing the surface of it with a spatula. Place the second sponge layer on top and brush it with the syrup. Chill in the refrigerator for 1 hour 30 minutes.

Roll out the almond paste and cut a round the same size as the cake. Lift the almond paste on top of the mousseline cream, decorate with a few strawberry pieces, then serve.

ne & Lili
Antoine & Lili

This cake, which was named after the Cardinal who served as First Minister to both Louis XIII and Louis XIV, was reputedly created by Jules Gouffé, one of a long line of pastry chefs and a pupil of Carême. Mazarin was also the inspiration for, among others, recipes for sauces, fillings, and lobster dishes.

Mazarin

•

Preparation time:
30 minutes
Cooking time:
30 minutes

•

EQUIPMENT

8½-inch (22-cm) round cake pan

INGREDIENTS
TO SERVE 8

- ⅔ cup less 2 tsp (4½oz/125g) superfine (caster) sugar
- 4 eggs (about 8½oz/240g)
- 3½oz (100g) currants
- 3½oz (100g) glacé citron peel, finely chopped
- 2½ tbsp (2½fl oz/40ml) sugarcane juice rum
- 1 cup less 1 tbsp (4½oz/125g) all-purpose (plain) flour
- 1½ tsp (5g) baking powder
- ½ cup plus 1 tbsp (4½oz/125g) butter, melted and left to cool
- Butter and flour for the cake pan

Preheat the oven to 400°F (200°C/Gas mark 6). Butter and flour the cake pan.

Whisk the sugar and the eggs together in a mixing bowl until pale and thickened. Add the currants, chopped citron peel, and half of the rum and mix all the ingredients together.

Sift in the flour and baking powder and fold in. Finally fold in the cold melted butter.

Transfer the batter to the cake pan and bake for 30 minutes.

When the cake comes out of the oven, turn it out of the pan, and brush with the remaining rum.

A devout dedication to Saint Germain, bishop of Paris in the 16th century. The almond cake recipe is said to have been created in Saint-Germain-en-Laye, a town on the western outskirts of Paris.

Saint-Germain

•
Preparation time:
35 minutes
Cooking time:
20 to 25 minutes
•

EQUIPMENT

7-inch (18-cm) square cake pan, 1½ inches (4cm) high

INGREDIENTS
TO SERVE 6 TO 8

- ⅔ cup less 2 tsp (4½oz/125g) superfine (caster) sugar
- 2oz (55g) whole eggs
- 5½oz (160g) egg yolks
- 1¼ cups (4½oz/125g) ground almonds
- 3 ⅔ tbsp (1oz/30g) all-purpose (plain) flour
- 1 tsp liquid vanilla flavoring
- 8½oz (240g) egg whites
- ¼ tsp salt
- Butter and flour for the cake pan

Preheat the oven to 350°F (180°C/Gas mark 4). Butter and flour the cake pan.

Whisk the sugar, the whole eggs, and egg yolks in a mixing bowl on high speed for 3 to 4 minutes. Sift in the ground almonds and flour, add the vanilla, and fold in.

Fit a stand mixer with the whisk attachment and whisk the egg whites to firm peaks with the salt. Once the egg whites are ready, fold in the egg and almond mixture using a flexible spatula.

Transfer the batter to the prepared cake pan and bake for 20 to 25 minutes. When the cake comes out of the oven, turn it out onto a wire rack to cool.

NOTE: IN THE PAST, THE CAKE WOULD HAVE BEEN SPRINKLED WITH RUM ONCE BAKED, THEN DECORATED WITH A FEW PISTACHIOS.

Choux pastry

Preparation time: 30 minutes
Cooking time: 30 minutes

INGREDIENTS
TO MAKE 20 CHOUX BUNS
2 INCHES (5CM) IN DIAMETER

½ cup (4½fl oz/125ml) whole milk
½ cup (4½fl oz/125ml) water
½ cup plus 1 tbsp (3½oz/100g) butter
1¼ tsp (5g) salt
1¼ tsp (5g) sugar
1 cup plus 2 tbsp (5½oz/150g) all-purpose (plain) flour
9oz (250g) eggs, beaten

Preheat the oven to 400°F (200°C/Gas mark 6).

Bring the milk, water, butter, salt, and sugar to the boil in a saucepan. Remove the pan from the heat and add the flour all in one go, mixing it in with a spatula. Put the pan back over a medium heat and dry out the dough for about 10 seconds.

Scrape the dough into a mixing bowl (to stop the cooking). Using a spatula, gradually beat in the eggs in three batches, checking the consistency as you go. If you trace a groove in the dough, it should close up slowly. From here, either continue with the recipe below or refer back to your chosen recipe for instructions in shaping the choux batter.

Line a baking sheet with baking parchment. Spoon the dough into a piping bag fitted with a plain ½-inch (12-mm) tip and pipe mounds onto the sheet, spacing them well apart. Bake for 30 minutes. Do not open the oven door while the choux buns are baking, as you risk them collapsing. At the end of the cooking time, prop the door open with a wooden spoon and leave for 3 to 4 minutes to dry out the choux buns before removing them from the oven.

Puff pastry

Preparation time: 45 minutes
Chilling time: 12 hours

INGREDIENTS
TO MAKE 2LB 11OZ (1.2KG) PASTRY

2½ tsp (⅓oz/10g) salt
1 cup (9fl oz/250ml) cold water
3¾ cups (1lb 2oz/500g) T55 flour
5 tbsp (2½oz/75g) butter, melted and cooled
1¾ cups (14oz/400g) butter in one block, for laminating

Fit a stand mixer with the dough hook attachment. Dissolve the salt in the cold water. Add the flour, salted water, and melted butter to the mixer bowl and mix for about 30 seconds to make a dough. Shape the dough into a ball, and cut a cross in the top. Wrap the dough in plastic wrap (cling film) and chill in the refrigerator for 4 hours.

Put the laminating butter between two sheets of plastic wrap and hit it with a rolling pin to shape it into a square. Roll out the dough to a square larger than the laminating butter. Remove the plastic wrap from the butter, place it in the center of the dough, and fold the edges of the dough over it in the shape of an envelope.

Roll out to a rectangle and fold in three. You have now given the dough one turn. Repeat the rolling out and folding and then give the folded dough a quarter turn clockwise. The dough has now had two turns. Cover it with plastic wrap and chill for 2 hours in the refrigerator. Repeat this rolling, folding, and chilling twice more so at the end the dough will have had six turns. It is now ready to use in the relevant recipe.

The key to making perfect puff pastry is to take advantage of the "helping hand" offered by using the best quality ingredients. It's equally important to follow the chilling times, which allow the dough to rest. You can prepare a large quantity of puff pastry and store it in the freezer.

Almond cream
or frangipane

Preparation time:
20 minutes

INGREDIENTS
TO MAKE 1LB 1OZ (475G)

½ cup less 1 tbsp (3½oz/100g) softened butter
½ cup (3½oz/100g) superfine (caster) sugar
1 cup (3½oz/100g) ground almonds
3½oz (100g) eggs, beaten
2 tbsp (¾oz/20g) potato flour
1½ tbsp (¾fl oz/20ml) sugarcane juice rum
1 tsp liquid natural vanilla flavoring
2oz (30g) crème pâtissière (see page 80)

Fit a stand mixer with the flat beater attachment and cream the butter and sugar together on low speed. Add the ground almonds, followed by the eggs, adding them a little at a time. Mix until smooth, scraping down the sides of the bowl with a pastry scraper or flexible spatula to incorporate all the ingredients evenly.

Next add the potato flour, rum, and vanilla. Stir the crème pâtissière with a whisk to avoid any lumps and add to the bowl. Mix all the ingredients together and chill in the refrigerator until using. The almond cream also freezes well.

Royal icing

Preparation time:
2 minutes

INGREDIENTS
TO MAKE 1LB 3OZ (540G)

3¼ cups (1lb/450g) powdered (icing) sugar
2 tsp lemon juice
2¾oz (80g) egg whites

Sift the powdered sugar into a mixing bowl and add the lemon juice, and then the egg whites. Whisk vigorously for 1 to 2 minutes. Be aware that this icing dries out and rapidly forms a crust on the surface, so it is important to keep it covered with a damp dish towel or plastic wrap (cling film).

APPENDICES

RECIPE INDEX

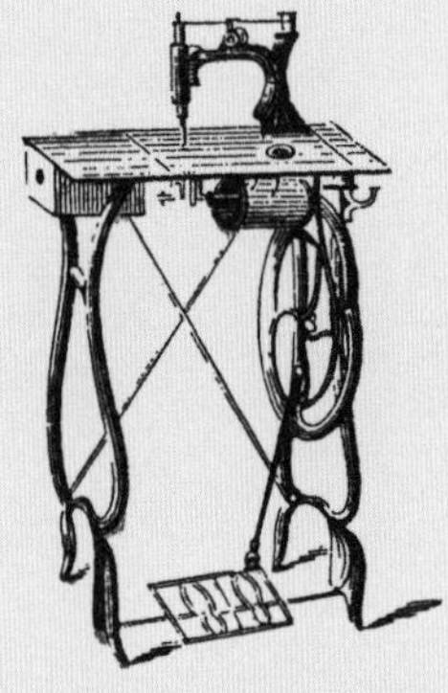

INDEX OF NAMES AND PLACES

FAMOUS PLACES AND FACES IN THE HISTORY OF PARISIAN PÂTISSERIE

Angelina

This celebrated tea room at 226 rue de Rivoli was owned by an Austrian confectioner named Rumpelmayer. Having opened several successful stores in the south of France, he turned his attention to the capital and, in 1903, together with his son René, he opened Angelina, naming it after his daughter-in-law. Actors from the *Comédie-Française*, Marcel Proust, and Gabrielle Chanel used to meet in the magnificent Art Nouveau rooms. Crowds still flock there today to indulge in the famous hot chocolate and Mont-Blanc.

Jean Anthelme Brillat-Savarin (1755 to 1826)

This Parisian gastronome, a lawyer and magistrate by profession, was also a distinguished politician and even a violinist. His most famous book, *Physiologie du gout* (*The Physiology of Taste*), which was originally published anonymously two months before his death, is one of the founding texts of gastronomy. Its full title is *The Physiology of Taste, or Meditations on Transcendental Gastronomy: Theoretical Work, History and What Needs to be Done. Dedicated to Parisian Gastronomes, by a Professor, a Member of Several Literary and Scholarly Societies.*

Antonin Carême (1784 to 1833)

Marie-Antoine Carême, known as Antonin Carême, rose from a very modest background to become "the king of chefs and chef of kings". Having served his apprenticeship under the pastry chef Sylvain Bailly on the rue Vivienne, he opened his first store on the rue de la Paix. A voracious reader of architectural treatises at the Imperial Library, he became famous for his spectacular *pièces montées* (tall pâtisserie creations). His fame led him to the kitchens of Talleyrand, under Napoleon I, who wanted him to develop a gastronomy suited to the way he conducted diplomacy. Invited by Tsar Alexander I and Francis I, Emperor of Austria, he also worked in London for the Prince Regent, the future George IV. He ended his career in Paris, where he was in charge of the kitchens of banker James de Rothschild. We have him to thank not only for the creation and improvement of many famous recipes, but also for the writing of *Le Pâtissier Pittoresque* (*The Decorative Pastry Chef*), *Le Maître d'Hôtel Français* (*The French Maître d'Hotel*), *Le Pâtissier Royal Parisien* (*The Royal Parisian Pastry Chef*), and *Le Cuisinier Parisien ou L'Art de la Cuisine Française au 19e Siècle* (*The Parisian Cook or The Art of French Cuisine in the 19th Century*)—true testimonies to his brilliance and the changes that were taking place during his lifetime.

Dalloyau

Charles Dalloyau, an *Officier de Bouche* ("chief taster" in English and an important role in the royal kitchens), entered the service of King Louis XIV in 1682, the first of four generations, all passionate about food, at the Court of Versailles. In 1802, his descendant, Jean-Baptiste Dalloyau, in response to the lifestyle that had emerged after the French Revolution, opened the first fine dining outlet at 101 rue du Faubourg Saint-Honoré, where he invented the concept of "take away food". It was here, at this continually innovative store, that the legendary Opera cake was created in 1955.

Ladurée

In 1862, Louis-Ernest Ladurée opened a bakery at Madeleine, a neighborhood of exclusive artisans. Paris hosted the World's Fair in 1900 and the nearby Madeleine was at the heart of the city's *Belle Époque* era, with women playing an active part in the thriving social and academic life of the time. Ernest Ladurée's wife, Jeanne Souchard, brought coffee and pastries together, opening a celebrated tea room where these intellectual exchanges could take place and, from that time, management was passed down from mother to daughter. In 1930, Pierre Desfontaines, a pastry chef and second cousin of Ladurée's founder, turned his expertise to creating the macaron, which is now the company's flagship product.

Gaston Lenôtre (1920 to 2009)

Son of Gaston Lenôtre, a *chef saucier* (sauces chef) at the Grand Hotel de Paris, and his wife Élénore, one of France's first female chefs, the pastry chef opened a store at 44 rue d'Auteuil in 1957. By 1964 he had established a catering business that helped build his reputation. In 1971, equipped with his outstanding expertise and his passion for passing on knowledge, he opened the École Lenôtre at Plaisir in the Yvelines, which has trained many generations of chefs and pastry chefs. Today, the company continues this tradition of excellence, counting among its artisans some *Meilleurs Ouvriers de France* (Best Craftsmen in France), a prestigious title awarded following competitions between professionals.

Le Procope

Opened in 1686 by a Sicilian called Francesco Procopio dei Coltelli, Le Procope is said to be the oldest café in Paris and one of the first to be dedicated to drinking coffee. Located in the heart of the Saint-Germain-des-Prés neighborhood, it was a meeting place for literary and philosophical figures of the time and its opulent decor played host to philosophers and writers such as Voltaire and Rousseau during the Enlightenment. Although ice creams, sorbets, sponge cakes, confectionery, and syrups were once served here, it is now a restaurant where diners can immerse themselves in the history of this iconic place.

Nicolas Stohrer

A pastry chef in the kitchens of the Polish king, Stanislas Leszczynski, who at the time was living in exile in Lorraine, Nicolas Stohrer followed the king's daughter, Marie Leszczynska, to Versailles in 1725 when she married King Louis XV. In 1730, he established the Maison Stohrer at 51 rue Montorgueil, where he brought together under the same roof the skills and techniques of the pastry chef, confectioner, sacrificial bread and unleavened cake maker *(oubloyeur)*, deocrative gateaux maker *(gastelier)*, gingerbread maker, and waffle maker, which had not previously coexisted. In particular, we owe him for creating vol-au-vents and rum babas, which can still be eaten in this institution near to the Les Halles, as diners marvel at the magnificent decor, which is listed today as a Historic Monument.

ARNOLD DELMONTEL'S BAKERIES AND PÂTISSERIES IN PARIS

Martyrs

39, rue des Martyrs
75009 Paris

Douai

45, rue de Douai
75009 Paris

Damrémont

57, rue Damrémont
75018 Paris

Lévis

25, rue de Lévis
75017 Paris

I dedicate this book to my children Camille, Paul, and Louis in the hope that it awakens their curiosity and their taste buds!

My hearty thanks go to everyone who made this book possible:
The team at Les Éditions de la Martinière who placed their trust in me: Laure Aline, Agathe Masson, and Marine Laurençot; Art Director Laurence Maillet; Guillaume Czerw for the photographs; Bénédicte Bortoli for the valuable information she provided on the history of Parisian pâtisserie; Stéphane Bern for kindly agreeing to write the preface to this book; André Oger for having allowed me access to the ancient grimoires of pastry making; My parents who have always encouraged me; My wife without whom none of this would have been possible. I would particularly like to thank all my teams and Chef Dylan Boedec for his contribution to this book.

My thanks also go to our growers and suppliers, because the quality of the ingredients we use plays a crucial part in the success of a recipe. These are men and women who look after every stage of production, from cultivation and harvesting to the delivery of quality products. As soon as I took over the *À la Renaissance* pâtisserie, I wanted this to be uppermost in my mind when choosing suppliers and my commitment to the quality, sustainability, and seasonality of the raw materials I used.
The ***Viron flour mill***, located in the heart of the Beauce region, supplies us with 100 per cent French flours, population wheat flours, and ancient organic wheat flours such as spelt, emmer, Rouge de Bordeaux, and khorasan, which I use to make my range of speciality sourdough breads.
In addition to being of outstanding quality and offering a range of matchless styles, I can be confident with ***Valrhona***® chocolates of the provenance of their cocoa and that it was grown in a fair and sustainable way.
By buying from ***Halles Trottemant***, I can choose quality fruit and vegetables, which they source for me from small local producers such as ***Jardins de Brière***, who supply the apples for my tarts and turnovers. When in season, strawberries are sent to me direct from ***Fraises de Mathilde*** at Plougastel in Brittany.
For dairy products, I work with the ***Laiterie des Bas-Vignons***, the last surviving traditional dairy farm in the Paris region. For four generations, the company has followed the family tradition of producing dairy products with the unparalleled taste of days gone by.
I would also like to salute ***Maison Déroche, Maison Delon***, and ***Patisfrance-Puratos***, all experts in bakery and catering products. They supply me, as do numerous artisans, Michelin-starred chefs, and *Meilleurs Ouvriers de France*.

First published in France under the title:
Pâtisserie parisienne (La). 70 recettes au coeur de l'Histoire

This edition published in 2026 by
Rizzoli Universe, a division of
Rizzoli International Publications

Rizzoli International Publications Inc
49 West 27th Street
New York, NY 10001

Rizzoli International Publications UK Ltd
Somerset House, West Wing
Strand, London WC2R 1LA

www.rizzoliusa.com

All the historical texts have been written by Bénédicte Bortoli, with the exception of the introductions to the neighborhoods (pages 23, 113, 143, 189) and some famous places and faces (pages 236 to 237).

Photographs page 238: Store sign © Arnaud Delmontel; portrait © Roman Jehanno

Publisher: Charles Miers
Associate Publisher: Tina Persaud
Production Manager: Michelle Wells
Senior Editor: Kristy Richardson

ART DE VIE EDITORIAL DEPARTMENT
Editorial director: Laure Aline
Editor: Agathe Masson
Assistant editor: Marine Laurençot
Head of production: Titouan Roland
Development and graphic design: Laurence Maillet
Proofreading: Sylvie Kempler

 A CIP catalogue record for this book is availa from the British Library.

ISBN 978-0-7893-4433-5

2026 / 1

Printed in China

The authorized representative in the EU for safety an compliance is Mondadori Libri S.p.A., via Gian Battist Vico 42, Milan, Italy, 20123, www.mondadori.it

Visit us online: Instagram.com/RizzoliBooks
Facebook.com/RizzoliNewYork
Youtube.com/user/RizzoliNY